Eating Disorders and Marriage

THE COUPLE IN FOCUS

BRUNNER/MAZEL
EATING DISORDERS MONOGRAPH SERIES
Series Editors
PAUL E. GARFINKEL, M.D.
DAVID M. GARNER, PH.D.

BRUNNER/MAZEL EATING DISORDERS MONOGRAPH SERIES NO. 8

Eating Disorders and Marriage

THE COUPLE IN FOCUS

D. BLAKE WOODSIDE
M.D., M.SC., FRCP(C)

LORIE F. SHEKTER-WOLFSON
M.S.W., C.S.W.

JACK S. BRANDES
M.D., PH.D., FRCP(C)

JAN B. LACKSTROM
M.S.W., R.S.W.

BRUNNER/MAZEL *Publishers* • NEW YORK

Library of Congress Cataloging-in-Publication Data
Eating disorders and marriage : the couple in focus / D. Blake
    Woodside . . . [et al.].
        p.   cm.— (Brunner/Mazel eating disorders monograph series ;
    no. 8)
    Includes bibliographical references and indexes.
    ISBN 0-87630-705-5
    1. Eating disorders—Patients—Family relationships.   2. Married
people—Mental health.   3. Eating disorders—Treatment.   4. Marital
psychotherapy.   I. Woodside, D. Blake.   II. Series:
Brunner/Mazel eating disorders monograph series : 8.
    [DNLM: 1. Eating Disorders—therapy.   2. Marriage.   3. Marital
Therapy.   W1 BR917D v. 8 1993 / WM 175 E14615 1993]
RC552.E18E2823   1993
616.85'26—dc20
DNLM/DLC
for Library of Congress   93-1238
                                                                                 CIP

Published by
BRUNNER/MAZEL, INC.
19 Union Square West
New York, New York 10003

Manufactured in the United States of America

10   9   8   7   6   5   4   3   2   1

To our families, children, and spouses

Contents

About the Authors

D. Blake Woodside, M.D., M.Sc., FRCP(C), is Director, Eating Disorders Inpatient Unit, The Toronto Hospital, and Assistant Professor, Department of Psychiatry, University of Toronto.

Lorie F. Shekter-Wolfson, M.S.W., C.S.W., is Head, Department of Social Work, The Toronto Hospital, and former Director of Family and Social Services, Eating Disorders Center, The Toronto Hospital. She is Field Practicum Professor for the Faculty of Social Work, University of Toronto, and Lecturer, Department of Psychiatry, University of Toronto.

Jack S. Brandes, M.D., Ph.D., FRCP(C), is a psychiatrist in private and academic practice. He is Director of Family Therapy Training for the Department of Psychiatry, The Toronto Hospital, and Assistant Professor, Department of Psychiatry, University of Toronto.

Jan B. Lackstrom, M.S.W., R.S.W., is Director, Family and Social Services, Eating Disorder Day Hospital Program, Adjunct Field Professor for the Faculty of Social Work, University of Toronto, and Sessional Instructor, York University School of Social Work.

Introduction

"If I had just had a bit more control over my eating . . . I think I could have
managed to salvage my marriage. . . . —Alice, at two years posttreatment

Long considered illnesses of adolescence, eating disorders are now
firmly established as occurring in adulthood as well as the teenage
years. As the chronic nature of these disorders is increasingly recognized, it becomes more apparent that a growing cadre of adult patients,
many ill on a chronic basis, will require treatment interventions. As
these young men and women move into their 20s and 30s, increasing
numbers will marry, and perhaps start families of their own.

These changes in the demographics of the population requiring
treatment and counseling have not always been met with similar alterations in treatment approaches. This is nowhere more apparent than in
the case of individuals suffering from eating disorders who are, or who
have been, married. For many years, it was generally assumed that people with eating disorders would rarely, if ever, marry, especially if suffering from anorexia nervosa; and while treatment interventions for
families, especially of younger patients, have been described extensively, there has not as yet been the same focus on the marital and
marriage-equivalent relationships of these young adults, and the very
special challenges and problems that they face. This volume is meant
to represent a start at remedying this deficiency.

While we feel that the assessment and treatment of such couples may have some features in common with the assessment and treatment of families of origin in eating disorders, we also feel that it is premature simply to apply existing family theory and practice to these couples. Rather, we seek to bridge the gap between existing formulations and our own clinical experience to present a formulation more specific to the nature of these marriages. We naturally acknowledge the contribution of the body of theory and practice relevant to families of origin, but hope to move beyond this.

Chapter 1 reviews the disorders for those who are unfamiliar with or have forgotten some basic information about the illnesses. We then look at the existing literature on eating disorders and marriage in Chapter 2. Chapter 3 attempts to make some links between the literature on family patterns in eating disorders, and presents a formulation for couple relationships that is derived from, but also is distinct from, these explanations of family interactions.

Chapter 4 describes our own format for the assessment of the couple with an eating-disordered member, and Chapter 5 gives a brief model of treatment for these couples that is suitable for many treatment settings. Chapter 6 presents some of the special difficulties encountered when therapists are involved in the treatment of such couples over the longer term.

We have a strong belief that the field of family and marital therapy, while rich in clinical lore and theory, lacks a sound empirical base upon which our theories can be tested and our interventions assessed for effectiveness. We believe that the field is ripe for a move toward establishing such a base. Chapter 7 presents preliminary results from our ongoing empirical research into the nature of these relationships. These data are not definitive: we hope that they will stimulate active discussion and perhaps other attempts to assess these couples' functioning systematically.

Finally, we address a neglected topic—the experience of these married couples as parents. Given the intense attention paid to mother–daughter interactions in the field of eating disorders more generally, it is a glaring omission to ignore the interactions between those individuals suffering from these illnesses and their own children.

There are several conventions in this volume. First, we have chosen to call those affected by the disorders patients. While we come from a variety of disciplines, all of us work in medical settings and we routinely refer to them as patients ourselves. Second, for convenience, all patients should be assumed to be female, unless otherwise specified; and this, of course, implies that all those described as spouses are husbands. We in no way mean to imply that males are unaffected by these disorders; rather, this choice simply reflects our own patient population as having been predominantly female.

The book contains a significant amount of clinical material. We have altered specific details of a given case to protect the anonymity of the couple in question, but have not fabricated cases simply to make a point. They all represent the real-life struggles of this group. The aliases have been assigned in a consistent fashion throughout the book— that is, when a given couple appears more than once, the alias used to refer to them the second time is the same.

This volume is an original work, and a truly collaborative endeavor. It could not have been produced without the efforts of all of us, and we have all contributed to each of the chapters in a significant fashion. We feel that it is appropriate, however, to indicate the main areas of creative responsibility for the book, noting as well the clinical setting in which each of the authors has worked.

Blake Woodside has worked primarily in the setting of the Eating Disorder Day Hospital Program at the Toronto General Division of The Toronto Hospital, and is largely responsible for Chapters 1 and 7. Lorie Shekter-Wolfson has worked both at the Day Hospital Program and in private practice, and was primarily involved in writing Chapters 4 and 5. Jack Brandes works in a private practice setting and teaches family and marital therapy at The Toronto Hospital. He was responsible for Chapters 3 and 6. Jan Lackstrom, also working at the Day Hospital Program, wrote Chapter 2. Chapter 8 was a joint project of Dr.

Woodside and Ms. Shekter-Wolfson. It must be acknowledged, as well, that Ms. Shekter-Wolfson initiated the collection of the data presented in Chapter 7; these data continue to be assembled by Dr. Woodside and Ms. Lackstrom.

D.B.W.
L.F.S.-W.
J.S.B.
J.B.L.

Acknowledgments

The authors wish to acknowledge the assistance of the numerous individuals who were helpful in the preparation of this volume. Shirley Sinclair shouldered the burden of the physical preparation of the manuscript. Drs. Allan Kaplan and Marion Olmsted agreed to the use of the clinical outcome data presented as part of Chapters 7 and 8. Dr. Olmsted also designed the statistical analysis, which was performed by Margus Heinmaa. Finally, Susan Brandes provided much-appreciated editorial suggestions.

Eating Disorders and Marriage

THE COUPLE IN FOCUS

1

Overview of Anorexia Nervosa and Bulimia Nervosa

This chapter introduces the eating disorders anorexia nervosa (AN) and bulimia nervosa (BN) to those who have not been trained in their treatment and etiology. The conceptual framework presented has guided the development of our marital interventions; therefore, even those with experience in the assessment and treatment of these disorders will want to review the section on etiology, in order to become familiar with our basic assumptions.

CLINICAL FEATURES

Table 1.1 presents the DSM-III-R diagnostic criteria for AN and BN (American Psychiatric Association, 1987). Anorexia nervosa is characterized by a relentless drive for thinness and by a body image distortion, which typically leads individuals to reach very low body weights. Patients may achieve these low weights by strict dieting, excessive exercising, or purging behaviors, such as vomiting or laxative use (Kaplan & Woodside, 1987).

Many of the typical features of AN are closely related to the starved state, as has been demonstrated by the work of Keys et al. (1950) and more recently, Fichter and Pirke (1984). These features include the

TABLE 1.1.
Diagnostic Criteria for Anorexia Nervosa and Bulimia Nervosa

For AN

1. Refusal to maintain body weight over a minimal normal weight for age and height; i.e., weight loss leading to maintenance of body weight 15% below that expected, or failure to make expected weight gain during period of growth, leading to body weight 15% below that expected
2. Intense fear of gaining weight or becoming fat, even though underweight
3. Disturbance in the way in which one's body weight, size, or shape is experienced; e.g., the person claims to "feel fat" even when emaciated, believes that one area of the body is "too fat" even when obviously underweight
4. In females, absence of at least three consecutive menstrual cycles when otherwise expected to occur

For BN

1. Recurrent episodes of binge eating
2. A feeling of lack of control over eating behavior during the eating binges
3. Regular use of either self-induced vomiting, laxatives or diuretics, strict dieting or fasting, or vigorous exercise to prevent weight gain
4. A minimum average of two binge eating episodes a week for at least three months
5. Persistent overconcern with weight and shape

intense preoccupation with food that most anorexics experience, and physical symptoms, such as bloating, early satiety, bradycardia, and ammenorhea. Also included are many psychological changes, including irritability, lability of mood, depression, and exacerbations of premorbid personality traits. Many individuals experience extreme social isolation as a consequence of their starved states. Table 1.2 lists some common side effects of starvation.

Bulimia nervosa is characterized by bingeing; that is, the consumption of large quantities of food in a short time. Clinicians occasionally confuse the presence of vomiting, a common symptom of bulimia, with bulimia itself: however, only about 80% of bulimics actually vomit, with the remainder purging through other means, such as laxatives, strict fasting, diuretics, or vigorous exercise. The typical eating patterns of most patients with BN include strict dieting between binges: some patients develop a chaotic eating pattern in which there are no periods of even relatively normal eating, but only continuous bingeing. In addition to bingeing, which must occur at a specific frequency,

TABLE 1.2.
Common Side Effects of Starvation

Dermatologic	Cardiovascular	Gastrointestinal
Dry skin	Bradycardia	Delayed gastric
Thinning hair	Hypotension	emptying
Lanugo hair	Peripheral edema	Bloating
Cyanosis	Arrhythmias	Early satiety
Carotene pig-		Constipation
mentation		

Endocrine	Musculoskeletal	Cognitive and Behavioral
Amenorrhea	Weakness	Depression
Hypothermia	Osteoporosis	Poor concentration
		Food preoccupation
		Impaired sleep
		Decreased libido

bulimics share with anorexics an intense preoccupation with weight and body shape. It should be noted that BN may occur at any weight, and that if it arises in the context of AN, both diagnoses should be made.

There are numerous complications of BN that are related to the bingeing and purging behaviors. Swollen parotid glands result from local irritation by hydrochloric acid during vomiting. Russell's sign (Russell, 1979), a callus or sore on the back of the hand, is secondary to abrasion of the back of the knuckles during the manual induction of vomiting. Patients who vomit frequently may develop severe dental caries, as tooth enamel may be quite sensitive to the action of gastric acids. Lacerations of the esophagus may occur, resulting in blood in the vomitus. Bulimic patients tend to experience the same bloating as patients with AN, but may not have early satiety. Patients who abuse laxatives may experience alternating periods of diarrhea and constipation, and sometimes bloody stools. In extreme cases, individuals who use large quantities of laxatives may become laxative dependent, unable to have normal bowel movements without the aid of purgative laxatives.

Individuals who purge via vomiting, laxative abuse, or the abuse of diuretics may experience hypokalemia; that is, a low level of the body salt potassium. Critical for normal heart function, potassium deficiency can lead to death, sometimes with minimal warning, and so constitutes one of the most serious medical complications of AN or BN. It is imperative that the electrolyte status of actively purging bulimia nervosa patients be monitored regularly.

The chaotic eating patterns in BN have a variety of psychological effects, including lability of mood, sleep disturbance, decreased concentration, and irritability. These features occasionally can be confused with depressive episodes; the diagnosis of depression must be made with caution in the patient with active BN. Because of the profound effects of chaotic eating and starvation on mood, significant suicidal ideation may be seen in some patients.

Despite the above caution, there is considerable psychiatric comorbidity in these individuals. The majority of patients with BN will report a lifetime history of at least one episode of depression, and nearly 50% will have experienced difficulty with a substance, most commonly alcohol. Less frequent are the diagnoses of anxiety disorders or bipolar affective disorder. In our experience, the diagnosis of schizophrenia is rare in patients with either AN or BN.

Patients suffering from both of these disorders may experience very marked distortions in the perceptions of their bodies. These concerns tend to persist well beyond the point at which eating is normalized, most likely representing a major contributor to relapse. The concerns may be relatively unfocused, appearing to have little referent in the patient's life, or they may be related very distinctly to particular traumatic events, such as childhood sexual or physical abuse.

EPIDEMIOLOGY

Anorexia nervosa is thought to occur in approximately 0.5–1% of women aged 15–40 (Crisp, Palmer, & Kaluci, 1976). Rare cases of late onset have been reported (Hsu & Zimmer, 1988). Bulimia nervosa probably is found in a slightly higher percentage, perhaps as much as

1–2% of the same age grouping (Fairburn & Beglin, 1990). The symptom of binge eating is fairly common, in both men and women: however, this symptom alone should not be confused with the full-syndrome illness, which requires the excessive preoccupation with weight and shape described above.

Male cases account for about 5% of most series, with BN being much more prevalent than AN. The reason for the predominance of female cases is unknown, but may well relate to the differential dosing that men and women receive in terms of the cultural message to achieve slimness. It may also be that other, as yet undetermined, constitutional factors play some part. In any event, no significant differences have been demonstrated between male and female cases, and the two situations should be treated in the same manner.

ETIOLOGY

No definitive etiology has been demonstrated for either AN or BN. At present, a multidetermined model, such as that advocated by Garfinkel and Garner (1982), seems most appropriate in furthering our understanding of these complex conditions. In this model, each person experiences a range of specific predisposing factors, which may include all of the psychological factors, biological factors, social factors, and family factors. Some typical issues that are common antecedents to the development of an eating disorder are presented in Table 1.3. Dally (1984) believes that marital discord is an important precipitant for AN that develops in adult life. Common threads in these issues are a sense of impaired self-worth and a feeling of ineffectiveness or of being out of control. The model suggest that these feelings may lead some individuals to engage in dieting behaviors as a way to regain a sense of control and temporarily to elevate self-esteem.

Unfortunately, dieting and losing weight are not likely to be an effective approach to resolving psychological difficulties in the long run. Figure 1.1 demonstrates the ways in which dieting behaviors become

TABLE 1.3.
Common Antecedents to the Development of an Eating Disorder

Individual
- Autonomy, identity, and separation concerns
- Perceptual disturbances
- Weight preoccupation
- Cognitive disturbances
- Chronic medical illnesses (IDDM)

Family
- Inherited biologic predisposition
    Family history of eating disorders
    Family history of alcoholism, affective illness
    Family history of obesity (bulimia)
- Magnification of cultural factors
- Parent–Child interactions leading to problems with autonomy and separation

Cultural
- Pressures for thinness
- Pressures for performance

problems for patients with eating disorders. First, as the dieting behavior does not resolve psychological problems, it must continue for the individual to maintain a feeling of well-being. This factor in itself creates a vicious circle, as the effect of long-term dieting is almost invariably weight gain (for a review, see Ciliska, 1991, pp. 3–21). For a small percentage of individuals, ongoing dieting with continued weight loss to the point of emaciation occurs, resulting in AN. Many specific effects of starvation, such as bloating, early satiety, and ankle edema, may directly lead the patient with AN to restrain her food intake further in an effort to reverse the starvation effect. The severe effects of starvation and chaotic eating on the vocational and relationship spheres of these patients further contribute to their sense of ineffectiveness and low self-esteem. For example, many such individuals are forced to drop out of educational programs or to leave their jobs because of a lack of the ability to concentrate. Some of us (Woodside, et al., submitted for publication) have noted the effects of active eating on family functioning. Why certain individuals are able to continue to suppress their weight to this point is unknown, but it may well be the result of

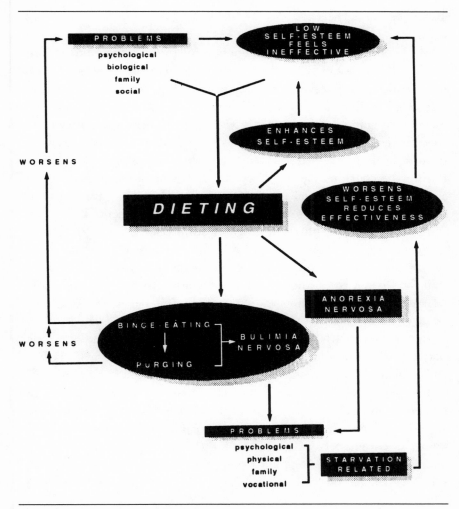

Figure 1.1. Formulation of Eating Disorders

some hereditary component. Eventually, as a result of the profound effects of starvation on physical and psychological functioning, an individual with AN may come to treatment. However, it is rare for the core symptom of the illness, the drive for thinness, to be ego-dystonic at this stage; rather, the patient often will desire to be rid of the complications associated with the starved state while still wanting to remain very thin.

More common is the development of bingeing in response to ongoing dieting. The work of Polivy (1976) on the determinants of normal eating strongly suggests a causal relationship between chronically restrained eating and bingeing behaviors. Once established, the dieting-bingeing cycle commonly will lead to purging behaviors or to stricter dieting to "undo" the effect of the bingeing. These behaviors, in turn, lead to increased starvation, and thus increased bingeing, facilitating the continuation of the cycle. And none of this contributes to a resolution of the initial psychological disturbance. In fact, once one has invested self-esteem into not eating, the development of binge eating is a devastating blow that, again, simply feeds into the cycle.

Viewed in this light, the application of models of addiction to the eating disorders becomes possible. However, it must be emphasized that food is not the addictive substance; rather, such individuals must be seen as having become addicted to dieting behaviors. It is these behaviors that must be targeted in treatment efforts.

In our opinion, the development of an appreciation of the connection between dietary restraint and eating disorders is an essential task for any professional who works clinically with patients suffering from AN or BN, regardless of the nature of the primary treatment that is being offered. Failure to have a clear understanding of these interactions may significantly impair the ability of a clinician to provide appropriate care for these patients. Needless to say, we do not support any treatment strategy that is focused on food avoidance, as such a strategy almost certainly will make both illnesses worse for the vast majority of patients.

ASSESSMENT OF THE EATING-DISORDERED PATIENT

Table 1.4 presents the components that make up a basic assessment of the patient with an eating disorder. Interested readers may also wish to become familiar with structured diagnostic interviews for eating disor-

TABLE 1.4.
Basic Components of the Assessment of a
Patient with an Eating Disorder

Overview and initiating factors
Weight history
Typical day's eating
Bingeing
Purging
Medical/psychological complications
Past psychiatric history
Family history

ders, such as the Eating Disorders Examination (Cooper & Fairburn, 1987). Chapter 4 details more comprehensive assessment techniques pertaining to couples. Practicing family and/or marital therapists may see many patients who have been referred having already had a general assessment performed. When this is not the case, we recommend that the family/marital therapist either perform such an assessment or arrange to have an appropriate assessment done. The reasons for this are many. First, as reviewed below, we support a multidimensional model of treatment, as well as a model of multidimensional causation. Thus our expectation would be that at the same time that family or marital therapy was occurring, other treatment modalities would also be employed. We do not recommend family or marital therapy as the sole treatment modality for patients with active eating disorders.

Second, both AN and BN may result in serious, life-threatening medical complications. Therapists who are not physicians should not put themselves in a position of feeling that they are responsible for monitoring these complications when they neither are trained to do so nor have access to appropriate diagnostic facilities.

The assessment has two basic parts: assessment of eating behaviors and symptoms and assessment of other relevant information.

Eating Behaviors

Overview and Initiating Factors

Initially obtaining an overview of the history of the eating disorder is useful, as it will assist the interviewer in focusing his or her questions more effectively. Such an overview includes information on the initiation of dieting behaviors and significant changes that have occurred since. Beginning in this fashion also may shed significant light on the actual predisposing and initiating factors for the individual in question.

Weight History

A weight history is very important. It should be noted that a record of height is a significant component of such a history. Patients with AN more typically will have weight fluctuations between average weight and a low weight, whereas patients with BN may show dramatic fluctuations in weight both above and below average. It is important to get an idea of premorbid weight, and this may be a convenient time to glean some sense of the physical size of family members. This may also be an appropriate time to obtain a menstrual history from female patients, including the documentation of oral contraceptive use.

Typical Daily Intake

The cinician should attempt to assess a typical day's intake for the patient. Some patients will be reluctant to disclose this information; others, especially patients with severe BN, may have such chaotic eating patterns that there is no typical pattern. It is wise to inquire about portion sizes, as well as the type of food eaten—some patients will eat very small quantities of a wide variety of foods. It is prudent to ask about foods that are typically avoided at this point as this information will be useful when assessing binge eating.

Bingeing

Many patients who engage in binge eating are profoundly ashamed of the activity, and will not always volunteer information about it. The decision not to probe into this topic may serve only to heighten the patient's sense of shame, and to drive the behavior further underground. We recommend a forthright but empathic approach, both in the service of normalizing the process of talking about binge eating and in beginning the process of promoting the ability of the patient to self-monitor. In this regard, questions about the onset, frequency, and initiating and alleviating factors of bingeing, including a description of what constitutes a typical binge, are appropriate.

Purging

A detailed inquiry into methods of purging is a mandatory part of an eating-disorders history, as it is purging behaviors that are particularly likely to result in significant medical complications. Asking about a purging behavior in which the patient is not currently engaging is not likely to result in the initiation of the behavior: information about purging behavior is freely available, and, as is the case with bingeing, the failure to ask about purging behaviors may simply reinforce the patient's sense of shame and inadequacy.

There are several particularly dangerous purging behaviors that include the use of ipecac to induce vomiting, which may lead to cardiac failure; purging by vomiting; laxatives and diuretics, all of which cause significant potassium depletion; the use of thyroid medication, which may lead to significant cardiac damage; and the use of amphetamines to suppress appetite, as these substances are highly addictive. It is important to ask about exercise, which may be difficult for some people as there is considerable controversy as to what constitutes normal exercise. Finally, marital therapists in particular may need to be aware that purging behavior tends to diminish the efficacy of oral contraceptives.

Other Relevant Information

Medical and Psychological Complications

A detailed inquiry about these complications will prove very helpful. First, it may alert the clinician to potentially life-threatening situations. Second, it also may help the patient to attribute to the abnormal eating behaviors costs that she had not previously identified. This is true not only for the physical complications of starvation, such as bloating and early satiety, but also for the psychological complications of abnormal eating, of which most patients are much less aware. This is another convenient point at which to assess the female patient's menstrual history.

History of Emotional Disturbance

This should include a history of both other emotional disturbance from which the patient has suffered and past treatments or counseling received. It is important because of the well-recognized comorbidity between eating disorders and other forms of emotional illness, especially affective and substance use disorders. Some patients with eating disorders will have received numerous other treatments for their illness, and it is usually helpful to discuss their expectations in terms of treatment.

Medical History

This should include information on significant past and current medical problems, including any medications currently being taken. The medical history may provide important information about the initiation of the illness as there are numerous physical conditions that have at times been thought to be predisposing factors for the development of an eating disorder (Garfinkel & Garner, 1982, p 182).

Family History

In the absence of a direct focus on family or marital therapy, a description of the structure of the family should be obtained.

Significant events in the patient's upbringing should also be outlined. For the purposes of this chapter, it will be assumed that a formal family assessment has been or is to be performed.

Other Personal History

An assessment of the growth and development of a patient with an eating disorder represents an integral part of the assessment procedure. It is particularly important to inquire about any experiences of sexual abuse, given its high rate in this clinical population. This topic is explored in detail in Chapter 2.

Recommendations for Physician Versus Nonphysician Therapists

Many therapists involved in the care of patients suffering from eating disorder are not physicians. However, physician participation in the care of such patients is often essential. Patients who engage in regular purging behaviors will need to have their body salts and cardiac function monitored on a regular basis. Patients who are emaciated may require hospitalization from time to time, and also require monitoring. In addition, the involvement of outside physicians may facilitate the counseling process if issues around medical problems have become a distraction in the counseling. Physician involvement should be viewed as collaborative: nonphysician therapists are urged to develop contacts with physicians who are willing to work in cooperation with them. The development of a stable, mutually respectful relationship with a physician may be an important task for the nonphysician when patients are considered to be medically at risk. This may also be the case for therapists who are physicians, but who do not feel comfortable in dealing with potential medical complications.

It is important that the development of such a relationship include extremely clear guidelines as to the roles and responsibilities of each partner in the treatment of each patient. Lack of clarity in this area likely will result in serious problems later on, as patients who are strug-

gling with issues of weight and shape may play one therapist against
the other. Each party must achieve a complete understanding of the
principles by which the other will operate, and while the goal is not to
blur the boundaries between the areas of expertise, each should have a
basic knowledge concerning the details of the other's interventions,
including the rationale behind them.

Although some of the stated approach may seem to be of limited
interest to the family/marital therapist, our position is that a more complete appreciation of the nature of the patient's symptoms is essential
both for appropriate family/marital assessment and for treatment. The
integration of this information into marital treatments will be discussed
in various subsequent chapters.

GENERAL TREATMENT STRATEGIES

This section is meant to provide a context into which the more detailed
information on specific marital interventions can be inserted. It is not
our intent to suggest that any given marital therapist should be able to
perform these interventions. However, as we support a multidisciplinary, multimodal treatment model for AN and BN, a general understanding of the more global treatment picture is important for the
marital therapist.

Interventions to Normalize Eating

As may be deduced from the discussion of etiologic factors, we view
normalization of eating as the essential first step in recovery from AN
or BN. In fact, we feel that in the absence of interventions to normalize
eating, it is unlikely that anything else will change for the patient.
This perspective does not devalue the many other factors that predis-
pose to, initiate, or perpetuate these conditions; rather, we feel that
abnormal eating itself is so significant in perpetuating the illness that
its correction is required as the first step in recovery.

Methods by which eating may be normalized are numerous, and no one method will be appropriate for all patients. At The Toronto Hospital, where three of us work full-time, we have adopted a stepped-care approach, wherein patients are assessed and entered into our treatment program at the lowest, least intrusive level deemed helpful, and then graduated through more intensive treatments as appropriate. It should be noted that we service only adults—that is, individuals age 18 or over—but that family and marital therapy is an integral component of all of our treatment programs.

The basic intervention in our program is the initial consultation visit, where a diagnosis is generated, our formulation of the disorders is explained, and a recommendation for treatment is made. Most patients are initially referred to our Eating Disorders Outpatient Program, where the initial intervention is a 6-week psychoeducational program. This minimal intervention has been shown to be effective for a significant proportion of patients, especially those with BN (Davis & Olmsted, 1992).This program, while primarily didactic, does contain a significant amount of group interaction, including an expectation that patients will disclose at least some information about the nature of their symptoms. A major part of the psychoeducational focus is on defining normal eating and providing strategies to achieve more normal eating habits.

Family and couple assessments and treatment are an important part of this program. Because of staff limitations, they are offered selectively. Patients who do not respond to the initial intervention are offered a choice, depending on their symptomatology, of referral to our Day Hospital Program for eating disorders or to one of a variety of longer-term outpatient groups. We do not routinely offer outpatient individual therapy, owing to the very large number of patients that must be serviced, rather than to a belief that such treatment is ineffective.

Patients who are admitted to the Day Hospital Program (described elsewhere: Piran & Kaplan, 1990) are routinely involved in family/marital assessment and treatment, where the goals of the treatment are somewhat focused (Woodside & Shekter-Wolfson, 1991; Shekter-

Wolfson & Woodside, 1990). Recommendations for further family/marital work after discharge are made as seems appropriate.

Finally, we also have an inpatient unit, which primarily serves individuals with severe AN. Family assessment and treatment are a part of the admission, with further family or marital work suggested when considered applicable.

While the programs described focus on normalization of eating as a primary goal, the identification of other significant psychological or systemic factors related to the illness is an important secondary goal. However, it is recognized that given the brief duration of the programs (usually around three to four months), the complete resolution of these difficulties is impossible.

We have discussed elsewhere some of the issues related to integrating family and marital work into these settings (Shekter-Wolfson & Woodside, 1990; Shekter-Wolfson & Kennedy, 1991). Chapter 5 presents a model of brief therapy derived from our work in this setting, and Chapter 6 describes a model more suited to open-ended outpatient treatment.

Although, as already mentioned, we do not generally offer individual outpatient treatment in our setting, it does sometimes occur. Our philosophy of treatment using an individual outpatient approach is built on the same principles as our other treatments, that is, a focus on normalizing eating combined with attention to significant psychological issues. We have found that if patients do not responsed to individual outpatient treatment within three to six months, it is generally not useful to continue with such an approach. In these cases, our normal practice is to shift the focus of treatment toward encouraging the patient to consider a more intensive treatment approach.

The principles of treatment to normalize eating include focusing on a nondieting approach to eating, facilitating patient self-monitoring, and providing psychoeducation.

Focusing on a Nondieting Approach to Eating

We believe that this is an essential component of the treatment of patients with eating disorders. To this end, providing patients with psychoeducational material outlining the effects of dieting behaviors on physiological and psychological functioning and describing the connections between bingeing and dieting is particularly important. It should be made clear that the intent is not to insist on immediate compliance with a non-dieting stance, but rather that this should be a shared goal for the patient and the therapist.

Consultation with a nutritionist who can provide the patient with a plan for normal eating is often helpful early in the process. A clear distinction should be made between this meal plan and a "diet," with foods from all food groups and a normal number of calories for the patient's age, height, gender, and activity level being incorporated. It may be helpful to deemphasize calories per se and focus instead on food groups and normal serving sizes. It must be stressed that treatment strategies that collude with the patient's desire to restrict eating are likely to lead to ongoing illness.

Facilitating Patient Self-monitoring

The gradual development of an ability to be aware of eating and restricting is an important tool for long-term recovery in patients with eating disorders. In this context, self-monitoring does not refer to the rigid and obsessional calorie counting in which some patients with AN engage, but to an activity that should lead to an increasing sense of mastery over eating behavior. Adopting an approach that emphasizes normal portioning rather than strict calorie counting will help to avoid inadvertently feeding into an individual's preoccupation with calories.

The more typical situation with a patient suffering from BN is for the patient to be relatively unaware of what she is eating, often because of the intense shame associated with bingeing, or because of the extreme degree to which eating has become chaotic. In these cases, self-monitoring with the use of some type of food diary will assist the patient in identifying the precipitants of binge eating, often taking the form of dietary restriction. As time passes, and eating becomes less restricted, ongoing self-monitoring via diaries or journals may allow for the identification of other environmental and psychological variables associated with either binge eating or restriction. The identification of all of these will help the patient to focus on the development of strategies to change behavior, thus facilitating the development of an enhanced sense of effectiveness.

Psychoeducation

Because of the widespread social myths about the effects of dieting behaviors, psychoeducational material such as that provided in the outpatient group described, is a vital aid in treatment. Accurate information about eating, body weight and shape, and the nature of the disorders is an essential tool for the therapist. Providing this information to patients helps them to become more active players in their own treatment, increasing compliance in the short term and facilitating an enhanced sense of self-worth and effectiveness over time.

Once the process of normalizing eating has begun, many other issues may become active.

Body Image/Weight and Shape

Most patients, even those who normalize their eating rapidly, will remain preoccupied with their weight and shape for months or years. It is important for therapists to recognize that the course of recovery given these concerns is prolonged, and, therefore, not to consider attempts at normalizing eating to have been ineffective if patients continue to grapple with these issues for some time. For some patients, the experience of being at a normal weight and eating normally will eventually be associated with a diminution of concern, whereas, other patients may require specialized treatment focusing on specific body parts. The latter may be more frequently the case in situations where there has been severe sexual abuse. It is essential that therapists be aware that concerns about weight and shape cannot be resolved at an emaciated body weight, even though many patients will request that their "body image" problems be cleared up prior to their attempting to eat more normally.

Family/Marital Relationships

As the issue of marital relationships and eating disorders will be discussed throughout this volume, it will be dealt with only briefly here. Therapists should be aware that the existence of a severely ill individual in the family is likely to have a profound effect on the nature of the family's interactions. In some cases, very severe family dysfunction exists, and persists after normalization of eating. In other cases, family functioning will improve markedly once eating is normalized. Areassessment of family functioning is necessary once eating is normal. If family or marital work is warranted, the focus of the work may have changed since the initial assessment. There is one methodologically sound study that supports the use of family therapy in younger patients after normalization of eating in AN (Russell et al., 1987).

Sexual/Physical Abuse

Research continues to indicate very high levels of sexual and physical abuse in both patients with AN and with BN (this topic is reviewed in Chapter 2 and discussed in detail in Chapters 3, 4, and 6). As is the case with body-image problems, sexual abuse issues are likely to persist long after eating has been normalized. Therapists who are not comfortable working with these issues may consider referring patients to specialized services, such as incest survivor groups.

Other Issues

The Role of Medication
Medication prescribed for patients with eating disorders may range from potassium supplementation to major tranquilizers (for a review,

see Goldbloom et al., 1989; Garfinkel & Garner, 1987). Again, it is important for physician and nonphysician therapists to work collaboratively when medication is to be prescribed so as to avoid therapeutic splitting.

Briefly, the following are the most common scenarios in which medication might be prescribed. When, secondary to purging behaviors, potassium is depleted, supplementation may be required, either given orally, or, in extreme cases, requiring hospitalization. Prokinetic agents—that is, agents that speed gastric emptying—may be useful adjuncts in facilitating the process of normalizing eating, as they help to alleviate the feeling of bloating and early satiety that many starved patients experience. In rare cases, various types of tranquilizers may be prescribed to reduce anxiety that patients experience while in the initial period of refeeding; however, this should be the exception rather than the rule, and they would typically be given only for short periods.

Many patients with BN are prescribed antidepressant medication. Ideally, such medication should be given for one of two reasons. Antidepressants exert an antibulimic (antibingeing) effect in about one third to one half of patients. This attenuation of urges to binge may help individuals to feel safer while attempting to adhere to a plan of more normal eating. However, it is important to be aware that this effect is unlikely to persist in the face of ongoing dietary restriction. Such medication should be presented to the patient as an adjunct to other efforts at normalizing eating, rather than as the whole answer.

The second major indication for antidepressants is the existence of syndromal major depression. The relationship between depression and eating disorders is complex (for a review, see Strober & Katz, 1988). Many patients who complain of "depression" while actively symptomatic from their eating may experience considerable stabilization of their mood once their eating is more stable.

Vocational Considerations

Because of the chronic nature of these disorders, many patients have suffered considerable disruption in their vocational life, having had to drop out of school or having lost jobs due to their inability to perform adequately. Some patients will benefit significantly from counseling, either to get their school plans back on track or to enter or reenter the work force. This can be particularly important when the individual has been involved in a profession that has heavily emphasized weight or shape, such as modeling or dance.

SUMMARY

This chapter has reviewed basic information about the etiology and treatment of AN and BN. A multidetermined model of etiology and a multidimensional model of treatment were presented.

2

Review of the Current Literature on Marriage and Eating Disorders

This chapter reviews what is currently known or hypothesized about the marriages of patients who have eating disorders. Our intent is to be comprehensive, but not exhaustive; readers will find that there are a great many issues that are peripherally relevant to this topic. Divided into three sections, the chapter first looks at the partners who make up the couple, followed by an exploration of recurrent themes, and then marital treatment.

THE COUPLE PROFILE*

Wives

The eating-disordered symptoms of single and married patients are the same (Heavey et al., 1989), with no evidence that the presence of a marital relationship alters the basic nature of the disorders.

---

*It will be noted that, for convenience, all wives are assumed to be the patients in this chapter, unless otherwise specified. The authors in no way mean to imply that men are not affected by these illnesses.

Van den Broucke and Vandereycken (1989c) reviewed 60 eating-disorder case reports and found that the average age at presentation for adult women with eating disorders was 40 years, but their ages ranged from 22 to over 60 years. Although eating disorders have often been thought to affect adolescent and young women, their presence is clearly documented in middle-aged and elderly women (Oyewumi, 1981; Jonas et al., 1984; Hsu & Zimmer, 1988; Kellet, Trimble, & Thorley, 1976; Launer, 1978; Crisp, 1980). The number of women developing or experiencing an eating disorder at an older and so more marriageable age is also believed to be increasing (Dally, 1984; Garfinkel & Garner 1982; Heavey et al., 1989; Hedblom, Hubbard, & Andersen, 1982).

Bulimic patients tend to be older than the anorexic women and are more likely to be married or have boyfriends (Beumont, Abraham, & Simon, 1981; Huon, 1985; Garfinkel & Garner, 1982; Vandereycken, 1988), though a significant number of anorexic women do marry (Heavey et al., 1989; Dally, 1984). Married anorexic women presenting for treatment are older and develop the anorexia later than single anorexic women, but also are ill longer (Heavey et al., 1989). The issue of chronicity of illness is somewhat confusing; it is a matter of some debate as to whether eating disorders occurring in the context of a marriage represent first episodes or the recurrence of earlier episodes (Dally, 1984; Vandereycken, 1988; Van den Brouke & Vandereycken, 1989b).

Husbands

The partners of eating-disordered women are described in a variety of ways from near-saints, giving generously of themselves, to disturbed individuals, suffering from severe psychological problems of their own. Despite this diversity of opinion, there is little doubt but that these men find themselves inextricably involved in their wives' eating behavior.

Foster (1986) views the husbands of eating-disordered patients as having a poorly defined sense of self-identity, which makes them similar to their wives. She believes that the overt helpfulness and nurturing on the part of the husband masks a profound need to define his identity through his involvement with a sick wife. Foster suggests that the husband remains invested in the eating disorder because the symptoms support his "false self." Further, she proposes that crises involving the escalation of eating symptoms or danger to the physical health of the wife are likely to force each member of the couple to face unresolved conflicts around identity.

Barrett and Schwartz (1987) describe the husband's need to have a "sick" wife in order to maintain his own self-esteem through the ability to tolerate or care for her. They believe that the wife's choice of such a husband serves to stabilize the relationship temporarily, as it initially serves needs on both sides—for the wife to be able to continue her pursuit of thinness and for the husband to bolster self-esteem by caring for her. Barrett and Schwartz suggest that demands for the wife to alter her eating behaviors imply that the spouse will have to be more responsible for his own behavior, finding ways to promote his self-esteem that do not center on caring for his wife.

Van den Broucke and Vandereycken (1989a,b), examining husbands systematically, identified higher levels of neurotic and psychiatric symptoms in the husbands than in a normal control group. Although these men were described as supportive and caring by their wives, these attributes appeared to protect the mutual dependency that had evolved between the partners in a superficial relationship.

Crisp (1977) describes the husband of an eating-disordered patient as having "very restricted and specific needs in life . . . he will have sought a perversely sexual . . . or an asexual, but still infertile partner" (p. 58). The pair are thought to have established their marriage in an effort to resolve or protect themselves from their own neurotic needs, and so will seek to resist change at all costs. These observations were extended by Dally (1984) who looked at 45 couples in which one partner suffered from an eating disorder. Many of the spouses were described as immature and doubtful of their ability to satisfy their wives or to keep their affection. The men spoke of their wives in idealistic terms, such as "sweet, understanding and forgiving" (p. 425).

Dally reports that the spouses experienced distress when this idealized view was threatened by either the emergence or worsening of eating symptoms.

Dally categorized the spouses into three groups. Members of the first group, accounting for over half of the sample, are described as emotionally and sexually passive, unable to tolerate disagreement, and actively avoidant of confrontation. These husbands find it easy to tolerate eating symptoms, as these symptoms reinforce their sense of being needed in the relationship. Even if there is overt marital discord, remaining in the marriage may be a more tolerable option for these husbands than leaving.

Those in the second group, comprising approximately a third of the men, were characterized by greater strength and an ability to avoid a mutually dependent pattern by enlarging their social support system. Dally observed that after an extended period of time spent trying to help their wives, these men became frustrated and angry and began to drift away from the marriage, either by becoming absorbed in their work or by establishing extramarital relationships.

The husbands who made up the third group were typically older than their wives, and many had been married before. The men were observed to be very controlling, expecting their wives to subordinate their lives to them. These marriages were thought initially to serve the husbands in that a compliant wife might bolster the husband's own sense of effectiveness; the wives, on the other hand, gain a sense of being taken care of by an older and wiser figure.

A number of common themes run through the noted observations, the most notable being the need for the spouse to make accommodations to the illness of the wife. Even when spouses make adaptive decisions, such as recruiting sources of support outside the relationship, these healthier methods of coping ultimately lead to impaired intimacy in the relationship. The dilemma remains: how can a mutually satisfying, equitable relationship be created when one member of the couple is chronically ill?

RECURRENT THEMES

Eating Symptoms as a Distraction from Other Problems

Many authors suggest that eating symptoms function as a metaphor or distraction for other problems in the marriage (Root, Fallon, & Friedrick, 1986; Schwartz, Barret, & Saba, 1985; Fishman, 1979). However, Foster (1986) suggests that this is more likely to be the case in marriages where one partner has anorexia nervosa (AN): she believes these relationships to be characterized by a higher degree of conflict avoidance, in contrast to the marriages of bulimic women, where she believes the interactional style to be more openly hostile and chaotic.

Levine (1988) reports that some of the small number (5 to 10) of couples she interviewed agreed that the eating disorder distracted them from their problems and sapped energy that might otherwise be directed toward other issues. One couple acknowledged that they focused on the eating disorder as a way to ignore other issues in their relationship. The patients, all suffering from bulimia nervosa (BN), agreed that as marital tension increased, they would binge more often. The couples formulated that bingeing had become a way of coping with marital stress. Schwartz et al. (1985) believe that bulimic symptoms are used not only to avoid feelings, but also to provide an internal sense of nurturance and self-soothing during periods of marital distress.

Van Buren and Williamson (1988) attempted to investigate conflict-resolution skills in bulimic marriages. With a sample of 12 couples, they observed that female bulimic patients used problem-solving skills less and withdrew from conflict more than the control group of normal women. Male partners in both samples were similar. The authors concluded that the ineffectiveness of the bulimic patients was related to their extremely low self-esteem. They were observed to avoid confrontation, with the result that they only confirmed their negative beliefs about themselves.

Family-of-Origin Issues

Boundary Diffusion and Replication of the Family of Origin

Many authors comment on perceived similarities between the marriages of patients with eating disorders and those of their parents. This isomorphism appears to have a number of dimensions. First, it is thought to reflect the daughter/wife replicating her relationship with her father (Foster, 1986; Schwartz et al., 1985; Kwee & Duivenvoorden, 1985). This dynamic is thought to reflect an underlying anxious attachment style, resulting in conflicts around separation and autonomy.

Schwartz et al. (1985) and Fishman (1979) describe how unresolved conflicts in the area of separation result in poorly defined intergenerational boundaries (i.e., difficulty defining hierarchy) and diffuse intragenerational boundaries (i.e., inability to manage proximity). This boundary diffusion burdens and ultimately threatens the marital system. Bulimic symptoms may serve to allow the patient to shelve her conflict about autonomy and separation by remaining involved with her family of origin. An oscillating pattern may be set up whereby the patient shifts between the roles of nonautonomous daughter and pseudoautonomous wife, which can be complemented by parallel shifts between the role of parent and husband on the part of the spouse.

In these families, issues of autonomy and separation need not be resolved because the daughter/wife is never required actually to "leave home." The nature of the marriage (e.g., poorly defined boundaries, conflict avoidance, inefficient problem solving) allows the wife/child to maintain her role as ill daughter and her parents to remain intensely involved. While such parents may be described as "deeply repulsed" by the symptoms their daughter expresses, they clearly have a high degree of investment in her symptoms.

Role Definition

Barrett and Schwartz (1987) address conflicts around separation and autonomy by defining two types of role complementarity that they observed bulimic couples to develop in an effort to "avoid role definition as an individual"—the "over responsible/under responsible" and the "mutually over responsible/under responsible"(p. 27) couples. These couples fail to develop a clear definition of self and take on interdependent marital roles in an effort to avoid definition as individuals. The mutually over responsible/under responsible couple must balance an alternating identity between that of caretaker and that of sick or troubled one. The husband, who typically is plagued by problems of his own as serious as those of his wife's bulimia, will only become symptomatic when it is his turn to be distressed. When apartner becomes overwhelmed, he or she is able to retreat into his or her own significant problem, and the other will switch into the caretaker/parent role.

Dally (1984) concluded that his married patients remained strongly dependent on one or both parents, continuing to use the parents' values and attitudes as their own primary frame of reference in daily life. They observed this pattern to continue regardless of the husband's values and beliefs and despite many years of living away from the families of origin. However, the patients felt that their parents neither understood nor respected them, and they reported hoping to achieve a degree of understanding and closeness in their marital relationship that had been lacking in their family of origin.

The Importance of Appearance

Little has been written about the value bulimic couples place on physical appearance. Root et al. (1986) and Schwartz et al. (1985) identify this as an important intergenerational factor operating in the families of origin and marriages of bulimic patients.

Levine (1988) asked couples about the importance of appearance and found that, in some instances, BN seemed to be selected as a method to maintain a particular standard of weight and shape. This is similar to the findings of Van den Broucke and Vandereycken (1989b), who discovered that values and beliefs about body image could be a significant trigger in prompting the eating disorder. They reported that physical attractiveness was important to both partners, and that it was an important factor in mate selection in some eating-disordered couples.

Power and Control

Many authors have identified issues of power and control as significant factors in eating-disordered marriages. Madanes (1981) and Barrett and Schwartz (1987) describe similar hierarchies present in bulimic marriages. The patient is cared for by her husband, who initially reports being relieved to learn what "the problem" is. The husband, who quickly assumes a superior helper position, is then confronted by the harsh reality of a partner who does not respond to his caretaking by getting better. This results in the initially more powerful "helper" being forced into an unexpectedly powerless position, whereas the bulimic partner becomes more powerful. This can eventually lead to the spouse's feeling entirely powerless.

These dynamics might reflect a female bulimic's ambivalent feelings about assuming power and control directly, as they seem to mirror the sociocultural struggle that women experience generally (Root et al., 1986; Barrett & Schwartz, 1987). The complementary dynamic, labeled in role terms as overresponsible/underresponsible by Barrett and Schwartz, becomes a functional way to mediate power and control in the marriage; neither person is required to take responsibility for him-/ or herself or for the relationship.

Root et al. (1986) suggest an additional possibility. They believe that the wife's BN can best be understood as an attempt to care for an insecure husband. By providing a major personal problem or flaw, she can negate her own strength and provide a means for her husband to appear relatively stronger. Such a couple can utilize bulimic symptoms to maintain a relational balance that might be endangered if the wife's strengths were acknowledged, or the husband's personal and social problems (which might include alcohol or drug abuse, vocational instability, or physically abusive behavior) were recognized. Such a marriage survives only if the couple can focus blame for all of its problems on the wife's eating symptoms. A challenge to this understanding of the BN may erode the foundation of the relationship and cause a serious threat to the integrity of the marriage.

When theories describing power dynamics have been empirically tested, investigators have often noted contradictory information. Levine (1988) reported on a sample of five couples, challenging the notion of mutual dependency. She found no evidence that husbands received benefit from the eating symptoms. Levine's couples reported that they felt their marriages had grown stronger and more positive as a consequence of the eating disorder. We wonder whether she might be describing a "satisfying dependency," the result rather than the cause of a relationship power imbalance, and thus a "benefit" in the relationship.

Van den Broucke and Vandereycken (1989a,b) support Levine's findings. Their research noted a hierarchical pattern of relating, but this pattern was described as a "satisfactory and cooperative" pattern, rather than as one causing frustration for the spouse (1989b, p. 184). They believe that the interdependence of the caretaking husband and the dependent wife maintained a mutually satisfactory dependency as opposed to creating a power imbalance. This is suggested by the observation that these marriages were rather distant and characterized by a relative inability to communicate about more intimate issues. The authors hypothesize that marriages in which a partner has AN might be more likely to develop a pattern of stable distance, whereas power imbalances would be more significant in bulimic marriages.

Avoidance of Intimacy and Sexuality

Most authors who comment on issues of intimacy and sexuality in the marriages of patients with eating disorders suggest that the development of the eating symptoms is connected to conflicts around psychosexual maturity. This formulation is often linked to fears about separation and individuation (Crisp et al., 1977; Crisp, 1980).

Intimacy

Van den Broucke and Vandereycken (1989a,b), investigating the communication patterns of 10 eating-disordered couples, attempted to measure intimacy by assessing the affective quality of the marital interactions and the accuracy with which the partners could describe each other's attitudes toward the marriage. The results indicated a cooperative relationship with a superficial pattern of communication, and the authors contend that the couples avoided intimate conversation. The spouses were described as more open in expressing their marital and sexual dissatisfaction than were the eating-disordered patients. Interestingly, each partner was able to accurately identify the partner's attitudes toward the marriage.

The modulation of intimacy in these marriages is described by Barrett and Schwartz (1987) as a process wherein the bulimic couple uses bingeing and purging not only to avoid intimacy, but also to maintain a connection. They formulate that the eating symptoms serve as a catalyst that brings a more distant couple together again, by allowing them to battle an external enemy—BN. Whereas these couples may be able to discuss personal and intimate issues when required to because of the illness, the very existence of the symptoms, the distress associated with them, and the attention they demand appears to preclude the development of a genuinely intimate relationship. If an issue becomes too intense, either party can withdraw with the excuse that the stress is making the eating disorder worse and impairing the stability of the relationship.

Root et al. (1986) formulate bulimic symptoms as a continuum of attachment behavior. Some couples remain locked in at one end or the other of this continuum, and others vacillate between levels of attachment. This vacillation is explained as a mechanism by which the couple can maintain marital intimacy at a level that does not threaten incomplete individuation and sense of autonomy. Specific patterns of interaction are noted by the authors. The overly close couple or pseudointimate couple initiate and then maintain their degree of attachment by working together against a common enemy. Partners who are more obviously distant from one another lead separate and individual lives, using out-side sources of support or distractions, such as their families of origin or work. For those who tend to move back and forth between too little and too much intimacy, Root et al. suggest that such issues as drug and alcohol abuse on the part of the husband may serve to regulate the tempo and intensity of the intimacy as these problems alternate with the patient's eating disorder as a focus for the discontent of the couple.

Sexuality

Crisp (1980) believes that avoidance of sexual maturity and its accompanying stresses is central to the development of AN. Although bulimic women are found to be more sexually active as compared with women with AN, they also report sexual difficulties (Russell, 1979) ranging from lack of interest to an inability to experience orgasm. Heavey et al. (1989) and Hsu, Crisp, and Harding (1979) found that all of their sample of married women with eating disorders avoided sex, regardless of diagnosis (anorexic vs. bulimic). Beumont et al. (1981) found that although anorexic girls maintained a wide range of experi-ence with, knowledge of, and attitudes toward sex, a significant num-ber had some sort of sexual difficulties. Crisp et al. (1977) and Guile, Horne, and Dunster (1978) suggest that the sexual problems of these couples can be dealt with using behaviorally oriented sexual therapy.

Sexual and Physical Abuse

It is becoming apparent that experiences with sexual abuse and vic-timization are common among eating-disordered women. Sexual abuse and physical abuse are not thought to cause the disorder per se, but these experiences render an individual more vulnerable to such an ill-ness, possibly by making the person more self-conscious about her body and by undermining self-esteem (Waller, 1991; Root & Fallon, 1988; Schechter, Schwartz, & Greenfield, 1987; Beckman & Burns, 1990; Calam & Slade, 1989; Bulik, Sullivan, & Rorty, 1989; Hall et al., 1989).

The percent of victimization experiences reported among eating-disordered patients varies in frequency, depending on research methodology, definition of the victimization experience, and sampling issues, with a range from 48% to 66% (Waller, 1991; Oppenheimer et al., 1985; Root & Fallon, 1988; Hall et al., 1989). Although extrafamilial sexual assualt appears to be more readily reported, on further investigation the incidence of incest is also thought to be alarmingly high (Hall et al., 1989; Beckman & Burns, 1990). According to Waller (1991) and Hall et al. (1989), bulimics tend to report sexual abuse more frequently than do anorexics.

The similarities of affect, cognition, and behaviors between eating-disordered women and victimized women are remarkable (Root et al., 1986; Root & Fallon 1988). Herman (1981), Brown and Finkelhor (1986), and Courtois (1988) describe symptoms of abuse in general populations that parallel those described by many authors in populations of eating-disordered women (Waller, 1991; Root et al., 1986; Root & Fallon 1988; Sloan & Leichner, 1986; Kearney-Cooke, 1988). Parallel symptoms include appearing powerless in relationships, susceptibility to further victimization, low self-esteem, feelings of guilt and self-blame, anxiety, hostility, depression, self-destructive behavior, body-image disturbance, difficulty in trusting, sexual maladjustment, and a sense of isolation (Schechter et al., 1987; Hall et al., 1989).

Bulimic symptoms are thought by some authors to serve as a method of coping with the emotional stressors that arise from the abuse (Waller, 1991; Hall et al., 1989). Anorexic symptoms are considered as helping the woman to develop a sense of control over her body, to avoid any evidence of sexual characteristics, or to deny sexuality itself (Sloan & Leichner, 1986; Crisp, 1980). The opposite course of action, to gain weight to avoid becoming sexual, is also reported (Hall et al., 1989; Goldfarb, 1987).

Brown and Finkelhor (1986) and Waller (1991) comment that incest may carry a worse prognosis as compared with rape because incest survivors may not have the support of the family to validate the experience and to assist them in recovery.

Timing of the Onset of the Eating Disorder

Many theories speculate on the role of autonomy struggles in accounting for the onset of the eating disorder. Some propose that women who develop eating disorders and subsequently marry continue to reflect unresolved struggles with autonomy from adolescence. Those who develop an eating disorder after marriage are thought to be reacting to marital distress, pregnancy, and/or unresolved, reactivated issues of autonomy (Andersen, 1985; Dally, 1984; Van den Broucke & Vandereycken, 1989a,b).

Levine (1988) describes five bulimic couples in which one member developed BN prior to marriage, and hypothesized that it represented a continuation of the adolescent struggles for individuation and independence. Three of the five couples confirmed the hypothesis, stating that the struggle for autonomy generally manifested itself around issues of power and control.

Heavey et al. (1989) studied 246 anorexic women, 21% of whom were married. From their observations, the authors hypothesized that developing AN prior to marriage or after marriage is more related to unresolved conflicts in the families of origin of the couple than to the nature of the marriage itself, and that the critical factor is the style of conflict resolution in the family of origin. Families of origin that use strategies involving distancing are more likely to permit a child to leave the home. The offspring of this type of family may appear to have greater independence, but this may actually mask a profound lack of autonomy. However, if the family of origin responds to eating symptoms that develop in response to family stress by rallying around the patient, she may be unable to leave the family or to marry.

The anorexic woman coming from a more disengaged family may develop AN either before or after her marriage. Heavey et al. (1989) hypothesize that this is related more to the degree of tension in the family of origin than to tension in her own marriage. If the tension is high and the symptom is not powerful enough to submerge the conflicts in the family of origin, she may have to leave home early and marry young.

High levels of tension in disengaged families may also cause asymptomatic individuals to leave home and marry early as a way of escaping. Further, some of these individuals may later develop an eating disorder as unresolved issues around their premature launch begin to cause tension within their own marriages.

Andersen (1985) believes that an eating disorder that appears after marriage is most likely a recurrence of an earlier episode during adolescence. He also believes that eating-disordered women will choose a "deserving" partner, meaning one less appropriate than she would have chosen if she had been well. Andersen believes that as the marriage deteriorates, the patient may find that returning to eating-disordered behavior stabilizes the marriage.

Van den Broucke and Vandereycken (1989a,b) found a distinct group of women who had a later age of onset (their early 20s), and concluded that the marital relationship contributed to the development of the eating disorder. Interestingly, the couples denied this, instead attributing the development of the eating disorder solely to body-image dissatisfaction.

Dally (1984) reports on 50 anorexic women who developed eating disorders just prior to or soon after their marriages. The women were divided into four groups: those who developed AN during their engagement period; those who developed AN during the marriage, but prior to pregnancy; those who developed AN within three years of childbirth; and those who developed AN at or after menopause. The women in the first three groups reported evidence of unresolved conflicts with their families of origin, and while they reported being highly influenced by their parents, they also felt very distant from them. These women reported seeking acceptance and understanding in their marriages. The women in the first two groups reported that the development of AN reflected a growing disappointment and disillusionment with their marital relationship, a relationship they had hoped would provide a substitute for the understanding they felt they did not receive from their parents.

Those who developed their illness around pregnancy reported a growing disillusionment with their marriages and an increasing sense of being trapped, which was compounded by the birth of their children. The authors formulate the eating symptoms as an opportunity to escape from these intolerable feelings.

The women who developed an eating disorder at menopause appeared to be responding to real or threatened loss, and their symptoms appeared related to depression, and perhaps to a wish to die.

Dally concludes that the first three groups develop AN as a desperate solution to a growing marital crisis. He formulates the crisis in the marriage as being related to earlier unresolved conflicts in the areas of identity formation and separation. Lacking a secure identity, the patients are ill-prepared to contribute to a healthy, well-functioning marriage. These observations and formulations are in accordance with Foster's (1986) beliefs about the role of the "false self" in women with eating disorders.

Pregnancy and Childbirth

Most of the literature in this area has focused on the effects of an active eating disorder on the outcome of pregnancy or fertility. Stewart et al. (1987) studied 74 patients with AN or BN, 15 of whom had had at least one pregnancy. Women who were in remission from their eating disorder at the time of conception had better pregnancy outcomes, as defined by birthweight and five-minute Apgar scores. Women who were symptomatic at conception had generally worse outcomes: the only two fetal losses occurred in this group. Eating-disorder symptoms returned in only a small minority of cases when the individual started the pregnancy in remission; however, most patients symptomatic at conception reported worsening of symptoms during pregnancy.

Lacey and Smith (1987) report a slightly different pattern. Describing a sample of 20 untreated BN patients, they note high rates of complications during pregnancy (although no fetal deaths), but record an improvement in the eating habits of most patients by the third trimester. In their sample, 5 appeared to recover from their BN symptoms after delivery; however, 10 of the 20 showed worsened symptoms after delivery.

Brinch, Isager, and Tolstrup (1988) report on the experiences of 50 women with AN. They note that the rate of fertility, as measured by the number of children conceived, was approximately a third ascompared with the local population; however, there was no difference in the rate of unwanted fertility, suggesting that the reduced fertility rate was voluntary. There was a sixfold increase in perinatal mortality, including five premature infants who died from complications related to their prematurity.

Numerous authors have reported on very small samples of patients. Milner and O'Leary (1988) report on a single case of pregnancy in a patient with AN who lost over 7 kg during the course of the pregnancy, and whose child died at one week postpartum. At autopsy, the child was found to have a significant cardiac defect. Willis and Rand (1988) report on a convenience sample of four BN patients, all of whom had satisfactory outcomes of their pregnancy. As has been noted in larger samples, most of the patients reported a decrease in BN symptoms during pregnancy, but only one fourth continued to be in remission after delivery. Treasure and Russell (1988) report on a series of six patients with AN whose babies all were below the third percentile for abdominal circumference at birth. However, these children experienced an accelerated rate of growth in the first seven months after birth. Finally, Feingold et al. (1988) report on a single case of a woman with BN who had a successful outcome of pregnancy.

Although the above samples are too small to be definitive, it would appear that the outcome for pregnancy is better for patients with BN at a normal weight than for patients with AN. In fact, no report mentions a fetal death in a patient with BN. There is a fairly consistent trend for BN patients to experience an improvement in their eating symptoms while pregnant, with a minority of about a fourth reporting long-term improvement subsequent to pregnancy.

Parenting

Despite the acknowledged increase in the number of adult patients with eating disorders and the increasing interest in their marital adjustment, virtually nothing has been written about how the existence of an eating disorder has affected the ability of these individuals to parent effectively. Given the enormous decline in other areas of psychosocial functioning associated with eating disorders, this is a germane issue.

A few authors do comment specifically on the parenting practices of these patients. Lacey and Smith (1987) report that three out of 20 of their AN mothers were slimming their babies by the age of one year. Brinch et al. (1988), reporting on a sample of 67 children of varying ages of AN mothers, note that most (72%) of the children had few if any problems with eating, and only two had marked psychological problems. One of the latter was a girl with AN, who died of her illness. It should be noted that the majority of these children were still at latency age, and that no formal assessment was done of the children per se, the authors relying on parental report and hospital records.

These results vary from those reported by Woodside and Shekter-Wolfson (1990), who noted fairly severe parenting disturbances in a sample of 12 parents attending an intensive Day Hospital Program for eating disorders. In this series, parenting difficulty was common with children over the age of three, and appeared to be correlated to the quality of the marital interaction. A significant number of this sample had become so debilitated by their illness that they had been forced to give up their children to the care of their spouses or other family members.

In sum, there is too little information available on the experiences of this population as parents. Clarification is needed as to what extent parenting is disturbed, and what factors exacerbate and mitigate this disturbance.

MARITAL TREATMENT

Most models of treatment for couples have been extrapolated from experiences in working with families. The main features of the authors' family typologic schema, which are reviewed next, are described in greater detail in Chapter 3. Although there are many differences among specific techniques, there is also significant common ground. First, there is virtually unanimous support for a multidimensional approach to the treatment of eating-disordered couples. This multidimensional approach includes using a wide variety of treatment techniques and models of practice, either concurrently or sequentially. Specific authors may advocate the use of systemic, structural, strategic, or behavioral interventions, but it is generally recommended that the preferred approach be used in conjunction with appropriate medical support. A multidimensional perspective both supports treating the individual, couple, and family in various combinations as indicated, and underlines the need for the treatment team to work collaboratively (Kwee & Duivenvoorden, 1985; Andersen, 1985; Hedblom et al., 1982; Barrett & Schwartz, 1987; Foster, 1986).

Indications for and Contraindications to Marital Treatment

Foster (1986, p. 580) is the only author who specifically identifies indications for and contraindications to the marital treatment of couples with an eating-disordered member. These are presented in Table 2.1.

The indications and contraindications presented are not controversial. However, as noted in Chapter 1, the profound effects of starvation and chaotic eating may appear as severe character pathology in the patient, and before this can be assessed, the patient will require at least partial normalization of eating. In fact, the majority of married patients with eating disorders are likely to be excluded from marital therapy if they are assessed while their symptoms are active.

TABLE 2.1.
Indications for and Contraindications to Couple Therapy (Foster, 1986)

Indications	Contraindications
1. Onset is at the start of the relationship or near a point of crisis in the relationship	1. Evidence of long-standing severe character pathology in the patient
2. Individual therapy is failing/has failed	2. Disinterest in therapy on the part of the couple
3. Marital conflicts are identified as a problem by *both* members of the couple (our italics)	3. Evidence that another form of treatment would be preferable
4. The husband appears stable enough to tolerate change in the relationship	4. Overt interference from family of origin (shift to family therapy)

Marital Assessment Formats

Several authors have developed specific models for assessing couples in which one member is suffering from an eating disorder (Barrett & Schwartz, 1987; Andersen, 1985; Foster, 1986). Table 2.2 compares these models.

It should be noted that the components of the assessments are influenced by the theoretical orientations of the authors. They are all similar in their focus on role rigidity and flexibility and the underlying assumption that the eating symptoms may be related to other conflicts. However, Andersen (1985) states that his assumption is that the couple is healthy unless proved otherwise. He prefers that the assessment include all members of the nuclear family (patient, spouse, children) except for those children who are too young to participate actively in the assessment process. He chooses to define the patient's current family as the focus of treatment, rather than just the patient.

Unlike Andersen, Barrett and Schwartz, Foster, (1986) first interviews the patient alone and then the couple together in an effort to execute a comprehensive assessment. She recommends the use of questions that reinforce the belief that eating disorders are a psychosomatic disorder.

TABLE 2.2.
Formats for Marital Assessments

	Barrett et al. (1987)	Andersen (1985)	Foster (1986)
Orientation	Structural (Minuchin et al., 1978)	Eclectic/systemic	Object relations/interpersonal/systemic
Focus of the assessment	Enmeshment/disengagement Protectiveness Rigidity Conflict resolution Autonomy from family of origin Social isolation Importance of appearance Meaning of food and eating	Interactional pattern Role flexibility Nature of attachments Family supports Current stressors Problem solving abilities Knowledge about the illness Communication patterns Developmental stage	Onset of symptoms and concurrent stressors Flexibility to disengage from focus on symptoms Function of the symptom
Patient seen alone?	no	no	yes
Medical evaluation?	yes	yes	yes

Goals of Couple Treatment

Levine (1988) sets three overall goals for marital therapy with bulimic couples: redistributing the balance of power in the relationship; helping the patient to reshape her relationship with her family of origin on the basis of a sense of adult independence, rather than of adolescent dependency; and expanding the couple's repertoire of communication and stress management skills (p. 103).

Andersen (1985) prefers to focus more explicitly on goals the couple has defined for themselves, including improving their communication skills, sexual functioning, marital expectations, eating patterns, and parenting skills (p. 144).

Barrett and Schwartz (1987) also outline specific goals when working with bulimic couples. These goals are similar to those of Levine, and include reducing bulimic eating and abstaining from purging. They wish both to foster the development of interactional patterns that are flexible and independent of bulimic symptoms and to promote the delineation of comfortable boundaries, as defined by the couple, between themselves and their families of origin. Finally, they express the hope that their treatment will allow each member of the couple to function more independently, facilitating a change in the self-perception of each individual and his and her role in the marriage.

Foster (1986) focuses on the function of the symptoms of the eating disorder. She says, "Marital therapy is useful only in so much as the therapist can get them [the couple] to develop a focus on the function of the symptomatic behavior within the context of the marital relationship" (p. 579). Goals include disengaging the couple from their focus on the symptoms, providing an opportunity to explore other marital issues that have been hidden by the system, offering the chance to decide if they wish to work on addressing any of these hidden issues, and helping the patient with symptom management.

Specific Treatment Techniques

Foster (1986) suggests a number of factors to consider when developing treatment strategies. These are summarized in Table 2.3.

It is apparent that Foster's approach is quite directive and focuses very much on behaviors and symptoms. Her recommendations address her major goal, that is, to help the couple redirect attention away from the symptoms per se toward other specific problems within the relationship. Finally, she emphasizes that the marital therapist, by setting clear and obtainable goals, is also limiting his or her area of expertise, and that issues outside of this area should be dealt with by others.

Barrett and Schwartz (1987), Schwartz et al. (1985), and Roberto (1986, 1987) correlate specific techniques with stages of treatment, as shown in Table 2.4. The authors caution that although techniques are associated with specific stages, they may be employed throughout treatment as appropriate.

Barrett and Schwartz's model of treatment is, in part, an elaboration

TABLE 2.3.
Specific Techniques Advocated by Foster (1986)

1. Written contract
   - Clarifies responsibility for medical management
   - Clarifies goals

2. A directive approach
   - Aids disorganized couples to focus their attention
   - May be modified for higher functioning couples

3. Techniques to address restricted expression of affect
   - Positive connotation
   - Inclusion of family of origin to broaden information base or to increase energy in system
   - Gentle interpretation of the behavior as protective

4. Techniques to address excessive affect
   - Active interruption of escalating interactions
   - Cognitive exploration of the ineffectiveness of these interactions
   - Direct confrontation of inconsistent messages
   - Direct skill training for improving conflict-resolution skills

5. Comorbidity/multiple problems
   - Generous use of referral to outside resources

of Schwartz et al.'s model. They direct the clinician to observe and track the marital interactions that appear to maintain the eating-disordered symptoms. The clinician explores the function of the BN within the marriage and within the context of families of origin before using structural and strategic techniques to intervene in sessions or prescribing

TABLE 2.4.
Stages of Marital Treatment (Barrett et al., 1987; Schwartz et al., 1985)

Stage of Treatment	*Specific Techniques/Tasks*
1. Redefining of the problem as interpersonal	• Establish relationship • Gather information • Acknowledge negative consequences of change • Restrain rate of change • Prescriptions
2. Changing existing patterns of interaction	• Challenge observed interactions • Actively seek alternatives • In-session tasks • Between-session tasks • Prescriptions

between-session tasks. At the same time that the content is being explored, the therapist must balance support and challenge in his or her stance while restraining change in response to the couple's ambivalence and natural fear of change (p. 31).

Barrett and Schwartz (1987) initially set the stage to create a context for change with the couple by defining the problem as a dysfunctional relationship process rather than as the "bulimic person." The clinician must establish his or her expertise from the beginning of treatment, and begin to set the directions for therapy and to challenge some of the couple's realities in a supportive, intellectual way rather than in a personally confrontational way. They advocate the use of journals and logs to track the correlation between symptoms and life events. They note that keeping a journal often causes a paradoxical reaction to bulimic symptoms and contributes to a reduction of the symptoms.

Schwartz et al. (1985) suggest the use of symptom separation as an important addition to this list of tasks and techniques. They view involvement in the actual symptoms as a distraction from other issues. They suggest that the husband's response to the prescription of a "holiday" from policing the patient may well be prognostic of the ultimate outcome.

An additional directive suggested by Schwartz et al. is that the patient allow herself to become depressed for a specific period of time about the things in her life that warrant such a response. The husband is directed to help by giving her privacy and by letting her be sad rather than by trying to cheer her up. The goal of prescribing a depression is useful, as it affords the patient some time to begin making plans about how to deal with problems that are unrelated to food and weight, thus allowing her to feel in control of her feelings.

Barrett and Schwartz (1987) mark the movement to stage two of marital treatment by the active use of the themes established in the first stage. These themes are used to challenge the interactional patterns tracked earlier, and to provide suggestions for alternative behaviors. The majority of sessions focus directly on the interactional patterns of the couple, the goal being to develop the new ways for the couple to relate.

In-session tasks focus specifically on communication patterns and conflict-resolution skills. These could include inviting members of the family of origin to a session to help explore their possible role in maintaining a symptom. Individual tasks may be prescribed to the husband and wife to help each determine the impact of his or her behavior on the relationship.

Between-session tasks are designed to address both content and process. These tasks should encourage the couple to work autonomously, provide continuity to the therapy, emphasize the content and process of therapy, and raise the intensity of the work done in sessions (Barrett & Schwartz, 1987, p. 37).

Eating symptoms are addressed more directly in this second stage. The partners are expected to generate new ways of understanding the relationship, and consequently to develop new behavioral patterns that exclude the need for the eating-disordered symptoms. Direct tasks could involve the development of alternative behaviors to bingeing and purging. Indirect tasks generally involve rituals, ordeals, and symptom prescriptions (Barrett & Schwartz, 1987). These techniques highlight dysfunctional behavior by exaggerating it. For example, couples might be asked to plan a binge and purge, and then to report on their thoughts and feelings about the experience at the next session.

Roberto's (1986, 1987) approach to treatment focuses on the belief systems of the couple and the extended family. The transgenerational belief system, or family legacy, is thought further to complicate the dysfunctional relationship patterns, as described by Barrett and Schwartz (1987) and Schwartz et al. (1985). By using structural, strategic, behavioral, and systemic techniques to address specific intergenerational legacies, such as family loyalty, the importance of success and appearance, the meaning of food, and the fear of conflict (Roberto, 1986, 1987), Roberto believes that it is possible to help the couple to develop lasting change in the relationship (Table 2.5). In addition to tracking interactional patterns, Roberto advocates for the identification of and positive connotation of those dysfunctional behaviors that are in compliance with the "family legacy." She states:

TABLE 2.5.
Stages of Marital Treatment (Roberto, 1986, 1987)

Stage of Treatment	Specific Techniques/Tasks
1. The fact-finding mission	• Gather information • Explore the extended families • Present the family legacy
2. The problem expanded	• Reframe symptoms as loyalty to the family legacy • Exaggerate the consequences of change • Consider inclusion of families of origin
3. The price tag of change	• Prescription of relapse • Crystal-ball gazing • Increase time between sessions

"Motivation for change is stimulated, not by intervention into the symptoms (e.g., the daughter's overinvolvement in parental affairs), but by repeatedly reframing the behavior within the context of the family's belief system and reiterating the necessity of the binge eating and purging within that context" (Roberto, 1986, p. 234).

In the first stage, "the fact-finding mission," the therapist gathers and integrates data about the family belief system or family legacy. Roberto prefers that the extended family be included in this assessment, if at all possible. She advocates acknowledging the high degree of caring, support, and sensitivity that all family members evince for one another.

The exploration of the family moves backwards in time from the facts initially gathered. Data used to formulate the family legacy include "somatic symptoms in the family members, acknowledged conflict between the nuclear and extended families and proximity of various members as well as the presence of 'mavericks' who have violated the family's cherished values" (1986, p. 235). Roberto begins to report observations to the family or couple about intergenerational enmeshment, oppressive interpersonal expectations, and the use of guilt or indebtedness as motivators.

The first stage concludes with the construction and presentation of the family legacy. The interpersonal patterns observed—triangulation, overprotectiveness, blame, guilt, isolation, and self-sacrifice—are reframed as "transgenerational values central to the family's sense of survival" (1986, p. 236). Thus the patient is also elevated from sick victim to "dutiful, but doomed child, fulfilling the family legacy" (1986. p. 236.). Roberto believes that this positive connotation of the family's behavior weakens the grip of the intergenerational beliefs that keep the family stuck in a repetitive pattern. Her belief is that a more direct approach—that is, directly challenging the passing on of the family legacy—is unlikely to be successful, except in cases where the symptoms are of very brief duration.

Roberto (1986, 1987) labels the second stage "the problem expanded." If the extended family has not yet been involved in treatment, she highly recommends their presence at this time. The second stage is used to increase the pressure to change. Roberto uses specific procedures to heighten awareness and pressure the couple to change. The procedures include reframing conflicts and symptoms as evidence of the patient's loyalty and self-sacrifice to the family legacy and using humor to challenge the themes seeded in the first stage. She exaggerates the consequences of change: "Tension begins to increase during this phase of therapy as individual family members must decide whether to continue this previous behavior (with a growing awareness of its linkage to the bulimia) or to abandon the old structure for a new one that reflects correct needs" (1987, p. 10). Generally, any evidence of regression is accepted as ongoing proof of the patient's loyalty and belief in the family legacy.

The third stage is devoted to the consolidation of change. It begins when the couple reports on how they have begun successfully to resolve issues between them. According to Roberto, the therapist's main task at this time is to attend to the possibility of relapse and possible future problems. Roberto calls the third stage "the price tag of change." The therapist belabors the practical consequences of change, including possible parental divorce, individual depressions, and loneliness, with the goal of energizing one family member to tire of the family process and begin changing. Because the pressure to change comes from within the family, the escalation of resistant behaviors is checked. Assignments used at this stage should be presented as tests to measure the cost of change for the family.

Impasses in Treatment

Roberto (1991) states: "Regardless of the treatment model used— behavioral, object relations or systemic—treating bulimia nervosa appears to engender specific therapeutic impasses that make the process of change difficult and the potential for relapse high" (p. 69—see Table 2.6). She describes a number of specific impasses that can occur when treating eating-disordered families and couples, dividing the impasses into two categories—those between the family and the treatment team, and those that occur among the family members. She views the impasses as "moves by one or more family members in therapy that serve to prevent the bulimic patient from disrupting the rigid, enmeshed, overprotective marital or family organization" (p. 71).

Couples may resist change through "strong mutual protectiveness" (p. 71), creating a rigid and impermeable boundary between the family and the treatment team. This type of couple will present with a strong

TABLE 2.6.
Impasses in Marital Therapy Related to Increasing Autonomy (Roberto, 1991)

Impasse	Features	Meaning
1. Mutual interdependency	Couple oscillates between helper and helpless roles	Couple is poorly differentiated
2. Rigidity	One partner refuses to discuss painful material	Couple fears dissolution
3. Conflict detouring/ premature closure	Patient rigidly cast in sick role: couple claims treatment is making things worse	Couple has poor conflict resolution skills
4. Disqualification	Threats, criticism, guilt induction	Couple fears increased assertiveness, attempts to delay change

reluctance to reveal any information. Couples may also minimize and deny stressors. Roberto describes the tradition of self-sacrifice, as described by Selvini-Palazzoli (1978). It is incumbent on the therapist to maintain a reality-based stance and to be able to clarify the significance of any family issue, including the eating disorder itself.

Changes may be resisted by the couple, who may devalue the change as insignificant or not good enough. Roberto views this type of challenge to the team as reflecting a couple's or family's need to be perfect. The therapist must avoid the trap of agreeing with the family and devaluing the efforts made to gain control of bulimic symptoms, and instead confront the family belief system in an effort to shift the family from a perfectionistic stance to a more realistic one.

Roberto (1991) reports that impasses focusing on body image, health, eating symptoms, and interpersonal shifts toward assertion are designed to pull the patient away from self-management and such skills as identifying and acknowledging individual needs. She describes the following four patterns that typically occur when patients begin to become more self-controlling and expressive.

Roberto has specific suggestions for making use of these impasses. In cases of mutual interdependency, she suggests that the couple's tendency to self-sacrifice and protectiveness can be used to encourage them not to give up when the oscillating is observed. Overt recognition of beliefs about family connectedness, and the reframing of these beliefs as valuable, may allow high degrees of interconnectedness to be gradually challenged.

For rigid couples, directives that acknowledge the power and threat of change can be paired with directives to move cautiously and to continuously monitor the stress of change, thus empathically addressing the couple's fear of dissolution. This concept is similar to that identified by Barrett and Schwartz (1987) and Schwartz et al. (1985).

Roberto views couples using conflict detouring or premature closure as attempting to protect themselves from the intensity of disagreement. She suggests that therapists positively connote differences between the two members of the couple and attempt to normalize conflict. She believes that this impasse should always be considered when a couple presents requesting premature termination, either because of increased pain that is making things worse rather than better or with complaints that therapy is raising old issues that have nothing to do with the eating disorder. Andersen (1985) suggests a direct educational approach with these couples, encouraging openness.

Finally, for couples who are disqualifying, Roberto suggests directly commenting on and describing the dynamics as they occur in an effort to counter the efforts to stall the progress of the treatment. By describing a dilemma—one with no immediate solution—the therapist is removed from having to take sides. The couple can struggle with the choice between becoming differentiated and tolerating more assertiveness and having harmony and an eating disorder.

Andersen (1985) has also noted that as the patient demands new roles within the marriage, it can be shocking to a husband who had previously functioned full time as a benevolent helper. He warns of the husband who has stored up his anger until his wife is well, and suggests that a supportive and normalizing stance will help the couple increase their tolerance during a period of readjustment. He notes that requests for separation or divorce can come from the husband or patient. Husbands often report that they have been waiting for the patients to get better before leaving the marriage, whereas patients report that once well, they find their husbands "unsuitable" partners.

Relapse and Prognosis

Relapse

Relapse of eating-disordered symptoms is understood in various ways by different authors. Roberto (1991) defines relapse as a behavior rather than an outcome, and she understands it as a treatment impasse as opposed to some kind of behavior unrelated to the couple intervention. She has observed that this usually appears in the middle to late stages of treatment, and is usually a message to the therapist that he or she is advocating change too rapidly and appearing too enthusiastic about small improvements. Roberto suggests the use of "guarded enthusiasm" when tracking improvements and questioning whether the patient can maintain the improvements she has made in the face of pressure to return to relating to her husband in old ways.

Schwartz et al. (1985) also believe that relapse is most likely at the end stage of marital therapy, usually presenting as the patient's return to a stance of social isolation, dependency, protectiveness, and self-deprecation. They suggest prescribing a relapse in an effort to guide the couple through such a crisis.

Root et al. (1986) make a distinction between relapse and collapse. They understand relapse to be a purposeful but temporary return to bulimic symptoms in response to stress, which is accompanied by the patient being able to develop an understanding of the meaning of the behavior. Collapse refers to a return to eating-disordered behavior without the accompanying insight and awareness.

Root et al. attempt to respond to collapse and relapse with prolapse, working with the couple to identify warning signs, develop a sensitivity to vulnerable situations, and thus practicing to cope with difficult situations without returning to the eating symptoms.

Roberto (1986, 1987) believes that the failure of many treatments to produce lasting change is related to models not adequately addressing the "entire understructure and ascribed meanings in the extended family system" (1987, p. 2). She believes that therapists who fail to assess for deeper and more hidden beliefs that are embedded in many generations and that perpetuate values, roles, and interactional patterns leave the client system vulnerable to relapse.

Prognosis

It is generally thought that married women with eating disorders experience poorer clinical outcomes than non-married patients (Hsu et al., 1979; Crisp et al. 1977; Dally, 1984). Crisp comments: "The marriage is . . . embedded in the powerful neurotic needs of both partners. Neither dares to explore change. Such marriage conveys a worse natural prognosis although we have had occasional success in treating such couples" (Crisp et al., 1977, pp. 58–59).

Possible reasons for poorer outcome in married patients continue to be a matter of debate. Several authors believe that because married women tend to be older and often have experienced a more chronic course of illness, the chronicity, degree, and stage of the illness adversely affect the probability of clinical recovery and the prognosis for the relationship (Crisp et al., 1977; Hsu et al., 1979; Morgan & Russell, 1975; Andersen, 1985; Dally, 1984; Russell, 1979; Van den Broucke & Vandereycken, 1989b). Andersen (1985) suggests that couples who had a stable relationship prior to the onset of the eating disorder have a better prognosis and several authors believe that the maturity and flexibility of the spouse are associated with improved outcome (Dally, 1984; Lacey, 1983). Dally suggests that the weak, passive, kind, and tolerant husband, who is neurotically tied to his ill wife, colludes with her and actually perpetuates both the illness and the marital dysfunction.

Kwee and Duivenvoorden (1985) and Crisp (1980) report that as anorexic symptoms reduce in intensity, the marital relationship is increasingly stressed. Others have understood this phenomenon as the result of an escalation in hidden and unaddressed marital issues or as an effort to slow down a threatening change process (Roberto, 1991; Root et al., 1986).

Andersen (1985) believes that the best chance for successful recovery rests in the integration of individual and systems therapy. If the partners are mature enough, the eating-disorder treatment may provide an opportunity for growth and development. Successful outcome has been noted inn individual cases by Crisp et al. (1977), Fishman (1979), and Madanes (1981).

Support Groups for Husbands

Two reports (Leichner, Harper, & Johnson, 1985; Kapoor, 1989) describe and promote support group programs designed for husbands of eating-disordered wives. Leichner et al. describe a process group developed in response to pressure from a group of patients who felt that their husbands, though well-intended, were interfering with their recovery out of ignorance. The first two group sessions were primarily educational in focus, and the remainder became more supportive and interactive. The issues that emerged included a sense of personal isolation brought on by the way the patients coped with the eating disorder; frustration, anger, and guilt that accompanied failed attempts to help; problem solving around family issues; a need to develop strategies to cope with "intrusive, authoritarian, perfectionistic and unsupportive" members of the family of origin; a need for help in establishing appropriate boundaries and strategies for dealing with the actual eating-disordered behaviors and the recovery process; and a need to share their concerns about their sexual relationships. The authors noted that the men were surprised by how much their wives were similar to each other. Leichner et al. recommend the use of time-limited groups that begin with an educational format and then become more flexible as the group identifies important or shared agendas. The authors said they felt that the men needed help in identifying and owning their own needs and feelings, an important step toward taking increasing responsibility for themselves.

Kapoor (1989) reports on a more structured group that focused on a different topic each week, including understanding bulimia, healthy eating, coping with food situations involving the bulimic, dealing with failure to be abstinent, and helping the bulimic to be abstinent (p. 54). Among Kapoor's techniques were education through lectures, role plays, bibliotherapy, and homework tasks.

Both authors found the group to be valuable in a number of ways. Kapoor notes that the husbands were grateful to have a private and confidential place in which to discuss problems. The sense of isolation that the men expressed at the beginning of the group apparently ended as they became able to relate to others in a similar situation.

SUMMARY

This chapter has reviewed the literature on marriages in which at least one member suffers from an eating disorder. There is a remarkable lack of both research and theoretical material about these relationships. Although it is premature to make firm conclusions about the nature of these unions, the prognosis may be unfavorable in many cases. There is increasing evidence that the children of these marriages are also being affected by the illnesses and the accompanying dysfunctional patterns of relating.

3

Marriage and Eating Disorders: A Bridge Between Family and Couple Theory

Marriage formalizes a relationship in which a couple usually promises to provide exclusivity, love, and emotional, physical, and economic support for each other. In addition, there is generally an understanding that the possibility of having and rearing children will be considered. The context of this relationship, which includes each partner's family of origin, peer group, community, and culture, can either support or destabilize the marriage, but the couple itself must build its own matrix of trust through continuous negotiation of boundaries, rights, and responsibilities. In this era of unsettled values, fluid social groups, and disrupted extended families, marriage receives little enough contextual support, and is a formidable undertaking for any couple to entertain.

When a couple with an eating-disordered member deals with the usual difficulties that are part of any marriage, problems specific to eating disorders and other forms of chronic illness make the marital alliance an even more complex process. In this chapter, we explore how some of the dynamics of the eating-disordered individual's family of origin affect the newly created nuclear family. The discussion provides the basis for presenting our therapeutic approach to the marital problems of eating-disordered individuals. In addition, we outline some of the variables that handicap this unique marital partnership and contribute to some of the difficulties these couples face.

FAMILY-OF-ORIGIN DYNAMICS

Behavioral Patterns in the Eating-Disordered Nuclear Family

Descriptions of interaction in families with eating-disordered members include such behavioral patterns as enmeshment, lack of conflict resolution, rigidity, overprotectiveness, and the involvement of the patient in overt or covert parental conflict (Minuchin, 1974; Minuchin, Rosman, & Baker 1978). Kog and Vandereycken's (1985) review of the research literature on the families of eating-disordered individuals echoes these findings, showing a high incidence of controlling interdependent relationships and parental discord. Schwartz et al. (1985) note that, in addition to the above-mentioned behavioral characteristics, these families tend to be socially isolated, are overly conscious of appearance, and attach special meaning to food. Igoin-Apfelbaum's (1985) study of 21 bulimic women focuses on the history of the eating-disordered individual's family of origin, and, as well as reporting the enmeshment and isolation characteristic of these family groups, describes a significant degree of separation and loss experience. Finally, Selvini-Palazzoli (1978), Selvini-Palazzoli and Viaro (1988), and Stierlin and Weber (1989) also confirm extensive interpersonal overinvolvement, a tendency toward self-sacrifice, and a lack of leadership by parents in these families.

Family Typologies

Both Schwartz et al. (1985) and Root et al. (1986) have proposed typologies of families with eating-disordered members (including anorexia nervosa [AN] and bulimia nervosa [BN]) that organize the observed behavioral patterns and histories into a coherent picture. These typologies are remarkably congruent as they all focus on similar interactional and functional patterns. They provide a form of classification that highlights the predominant behavioral patterns of these families. Each typology has three categories: Schwartz et al. list the "ethnic family," the "all-American family," and the "mixed family," whereas Root et al. describe the "overprotective family," the "perfect family," and the "chaotic family." Although these two typologies use different names, they are very similar in structure.

Schwartz et al. suggest that BN families of the ethnic family type are most concerned with ideals and values that represent internal, historically based legacies. The all-American family type is most concerned with external, socially based obligation. The mixed families relate intensely and conflictually to both internal and external ideals. Root et al.'s (1986) description of the "overprotective family" category parallels Schwartz's internally organized ethnic family. Their description of the perfect family as one whose responsiveness to external, social expectations for behavioral models is remarkably similar to the all-American family (Schwartz et al., 1985). The mixed and chaotic family styles are also parallel. They represent families with styles that combine both internally and externally organizing patterns found in each of the other two discrete groups in the typology (Table 3.1).

Schwartz et al.'s (1985) analysis focuses on the observed over-valuation of ideals in all three family types, and notes that the maintenance of the family's ideals are more important than any individual's personal needs, desires, or capacities. They suggest that this underlying

TABLE 3.1.
Comparison of Root and Schwartz

Schwartz et al.	*Root et al.*
All-American	Perfect
Ethnic	Overprotective
Mixed	Chaotic

attitude is quite rigid and requires selflessness and sacrifice to group values because of the family's pressing concerns about group integrity and cohesion. They propose that this might be the way these families solve the problem of social isolation and an internally felt expectation of dissolution or loss. Stierlin and Weber (1989) suggest as much in their study. All family members who wish to retain any form of connection with the system are compelled to become an extended, stable, nurturing kinship network, whether or not they really want to do so. Root et al. (1986), who have adopted a systemic, feminist approach in their work, also point to the difficulties that family members experience in the areas of personal growth, separation, and self-delineation as the result of family needs, but they do not speculate about the nature of these needs.

Attachment Dynamics in Eating-Disordered Families

In a recent paper (Brandes, 1991), one of us has suggested that the coping styles of eating-disordered families might be usefully understood in terms of attachment theory and a focus on the insecure attachment patterns evident in these systems. This would allow us to link the findings of family work in this area to attachment theory and research (Bowlby, 1977a,b, 1982) and to a typology that directly addresses the function and the possible treatment of the dynamics in these families.

Studies of attachment behavior and attachment theory itself (Bowlby, 1977a,b, 1982) suggest that unresolved losses create a situation in which at least two different types of response are seen when the attachment system is activated. In one case, attachment behavior is elicited more easily, resulting in an anxious pattern of attachment. In the second instance, there is a partial or complete deactivation of the attachment system, and normal attachment behavior is inhibited. This is called an avoidant pattern. Chronic states of loss in which there is no form of resolution can lead to oscillations between states of attachment system activation and attachment system deactivation; that is, oscillations between anxious and avoidant patterns of attachment. Activation of the attachment system through the perception (correct or incorrect) of denied access to a bonded other elicits behavior that includes anger, irritability, object seeking, hyperactivity, and emotionality. This has been called an insecure, anxious pattern (Bowlby, 1977a). Deactivation of the attachment system leads to affective coolness, object withdrawal, emotional distancing, and rationalization—an avoidant pattern. When the normal resolution of a loss is disrupted (for example, as a result of the lack of or suppression of a group-supported mourning process), an individual cannot proceed with despair and sadness and move on to eventually find replacements. Instead, the individual continues a displaced search process by tracking all remaining attachments intensely (anxious behavior), or suppresses the search process by withdrawing from closeness with others (avoidant behavior). All later attachments thus become insecure, as they are based on the previous learned experience of unresolved loss and the learned expectation that new connections will lead to abandonment. As a result, any new attachments are dealt with in either an anxious, clingy way or an avoidant, cool fashion. If the unresolved loss experiences occur early in life, their power to affect subsequent behavior is immense, as the cognitive and affective structuring of these experiences becomes the basis for all subsequent attachments.

Igoin-Apfelbaum (1985) has suggested that many eating-disordered families have a history of significant loss that predisposes individuals in these families to experience difficulty in adapting to the changes and losses that are part of normal growth and development. In particular, the shift from childhood to adolescence, a common time of onset of eating disorders (Woodside & Garfinkel, 1992), seems to be most trying. It is possible that the normal, often sexually motivated extrafamilial involvement of the adolescent in our society places stresses on a family system in which many of the members are insecurely attached because the adolescent's move for involvement outside the family may be perceived as a destructive threat to the stability or existence of the system. Another threat to the insecurely attached family may be marriage itself, which is often the trigger for later-onset cases of AN (Andersen, 1985).

This threat to family cohesion and stability will be expressed in a number of ways (Table 3.2). Ethnic or overprotective families exhibit the object-seeking anxiousness of an activated attachment system (anxious pattern) resulting from the experience of developmentally induced loss and the expectation that access to the departing child will not be available. In this case, the separating adolescent is not supported in her leave-taking, and her attachment behavior is actually stimulated by the fear and overconcern of her parents. The behavior of the perfect or all-American families reflects an avoidant pattern of behavior in dealing with loss: namely, coolness, withdrawal, and the lack of emotional acknowledgment that characterizes this pattern. This withdrawing, avoidant pattern paradoxically will also stimulate the departing adolescent's concern about leaving by undermining her security of attachment. Mixed or chaotic families will display elements of both patterns, possibly from the same individuals at different times, and thus elicit complementary reactions from the adolescent, oscillating from excessive self-control and compliance to "acting out."

Thus either interpersonal enmeshment and overprotectiveness or the lack of emotional warmth and spontaneity, along with self-imposed isolation and lack of leadership may reflect a family's insecurely attached state. The lack of leadership and conflict resolution seen in both anxious and avoidant systems reflects the inability of anyone in the family to take a stand and risk the possibility of loss. Whether overtly enmeshed or overtly distant, the family members have not accommodated a past loss, and that loss remains unresolved. It is of interest that families of bulimic patients often give histories of actual loss and abandonment, such as the illness and death of an important family member, a change

TABLE 3.2.
Comparison of Family Types and Attachment Patterns

Family Type	Attachment Pattern	Attachment System
Ethnic/overprotective	Insecure anxious	Easily activated
All-American/perfect	Insecure avoidant	Deactivated
Mixed/chaotic	Insecure anxious–avoidant	Oscillating state: activation/deactivation

in socioeconomic status, or emigration and subsequent social isolation. Histories of sexual and/or physical or emotional abusiveness between parents and children constitute another set of factors that can be elicited in these families (Root & Fallon, 1988), and clearly engender a pervasive sense of insecurity in the system. Whatever their nature, the losses and traumas are not integrated into the family's understanding of itself and its functioning, and they serve as invisible paradigms or expectations of insecurity.

The following vignette illustrates the often extraordinary set of losses and traumas with which such families cope and the tremendous compliance and parentification required of eating-disordered members.

Barb, a 22-year-old married woman, came for treatment while struggling with the possibility of separating from her physically abusive husband after one year of marriage. The onset of her bulimia, six years before her marriage, followed the death of her maternal grandmother, who had been a significant caretaker for the patient (the youngest child) and her siblings. Barb's mother responded to the death by lapsing into a severe, possibly psychotic depression. Barb, age 15 at the time, took on a parental role toward her mother, and at the same time became sexually promiscuous and eventually pregnant. The mother briefly roused herself from her depression to help arrange for an abortion, but remained depressed for more than two years. Barb continued to date her lover after the abortion, and they became engaged when she was in her late teens. He was physically abusive, and she subsequently broke the engagement, much to the dismay of her mother, who was not aware of the abuse. Within weeks of breaking the engagement, Barb began to date her husband-to-be again and was reengaged after six months. Her mother viewed the reengagement with tremendous ambivalence, questioning Barb's ability to make judgments. Barb was married several months later, at age 21. Her conflict about the marriage at the time of initiating treatment was that separation might be upsetting to her mother. She had been

unable to tell her mother about the physical abuse, and thus felt
that in her mother's eyes she would have no excuse for leaving the
marriage.

Shame in Eating-Disordered Families

The prevalence of shame and shame-related functioning (Fossum &
Mason, 1986) in the eating-disordered family supports the hypothesis
that the family system is organized around its pattern of insecure
attachment. Physical appearance, deportment, performance, and
demeanor are matters of overriding concern for many eating-disordered
families. In all probability, this concern with image reflects an excessive
vulnerability to shame that members of the family spontaneously report
during assessment. Shame about how the family is seen by society at
large seems to be central for the predominantly avoidant family (perfect
or all-American families). On the other hand, shame about being seen
as defective by a specific cultural group is more characteristic of the
anxious family (overprotective or ethnic family). The oscillating family
that shows both anxious and avoidant patterns (mixed or chaotic family)
is vulnerable to being shamed by its image in the eyes of both society
at large and its specific cultural group.

Lewis (1987) has identified shame as a central affective response to
the internal perception of social disconnectedness. It is the affective
response and monitor for our state of interpersonal or social disconnection. As such it is part of the awareness of our state of attachment—
much the same way that pain functions to tell us of bodily harm. Thus
shame is an affect elicited along with the activation of the attachment
system when an individual feels disconnected or abandoned.

The link between the affect system mediating shame and the attachment system is still unknown. Our conceptualization of the attachment
system, which until now has been described in terms of behavior, will
probably require an understanding of the role of affect in its functioning. Nathanson (1992) argues that the affect systems, including those
that mediate shame, are primary organizers and mediators of all behav-

ior and not simply a part of other behavioral systems such as the attachment system. This distinction will be of great importance in the development of our knowledge of the structure and relationship of these systems, but it is not crucial to the following argument.

Insecurely attached family systems may leave their members vulnerable to the continuous experience of shame because they share a working model of the unpredictable state of security in their closest relationships. As we previously noted, this working model is one of expected abandonment. Because the model functions as the template through or against which all interpersonal and social perceptions are tested, family members are likely to experience many interpersonal events as potential abandonment and loss, and as a result, undergo continuing shame and attachment system activation. The connection between abandonment and anticipation of loss and shame has been made by many clinical observers, including Lewis (1987) and Nathanson (1992).

The experience of disconnectedness and the accompanying shame and anxiety is mitigated in these families by developing strategies that allow for a sense of conditional belonging. Security is acquired through compliance with social ideals and standards of performance and appearance. Thus, in the eating-disordered family, the activation of the attachment system and the confluent shame comes to be avoided or lessened by compliance, which prevents the experience of rejection and loss while the family's legacy of standards and rules goes unchallenged. This precarious balance is upset completely when the adolescent begins her movement out of the family.

The Anderson family came for consultation when their 19-year-old daughter became overtly emaciated and was seen to be restricting her food intake. The onset of food restriction coincided with the daughter's moving out into a student peer group and meeting a young man who seemed to be a possible mate. Both parents presented histories of significant loss in their families of origin and of great success in their work. In spite of their relatively high social profile, they felt somewhat marginal in society, the values of which they adhered to carefully. The parents were children of impoverished immigrant families and both had experienced childhoods filled with humiliation and shame. They wanted to provide their children with the best possible childhoods. The provision of "good and healthy food" was an overt concern for the parents, and their daughter's symptomatology served as a shameful rebuff to that goal. Both parents had to be continually available and accessible to their families of origin, and they felt exploited by this situation. They expected, in turn, that their liberated approach to child rearing would obligate their children to "share their lives with them" and "have a different relationship with them than their parents and siblings had." The patient's mother had experienced sexual abuse by her father. When dating and sex came up as a topics for discussion, promiscuity became a focus of attention, although it bore no relation to the anorexic daughter's actual activities. All the children in the family were required to perform to very high standards, just as their parents had. Both father and mother were concerned that their children "should not do the wrong thing and shame the family." The anorexic daughter lived at home and contemplated moving out. The mother could not see her daughter as capable of managing on her own, even though she was a highly motivated and competent university student. At one point during the consultation when the therapist asked whether any consideration had been given to the daughter's approaching departure from the family, the mother told the therapist that her daughter couldn't leave because she was too sick.

Whether or not the family's ideals and rules are useful in the process of growth and development, the demand to comply with them is powerful. Avoidance of shame by compliance may ultimately be maladaptive, but it prevents the burning, humbling, isolating, and self-conscious experience of shame. In addition, the anxious irritability of an activated attachment system is avoided.

The specific shame of being too fat is a recurring theme in our society, particularly for women (Silberstein, Striegel-Moore, & Rodin 1987), and it is certainly a dominant concern for eating-disordered individuals, and often for their families. The fear of fatness and its anticipated affective and relational consequences is at the center of the bulimic individual's program of food restriction, bingeing, and purging. How does this fear of fatness and the avoidance of the shame of fatness serve the family and the individual? Is the avoidance of fatness used as the means to avoid rejection and shame, or, to phrase it positively, it is used to achieve a sense of secure acceptance and belonging in the family's social context?

For many eating-disordered individuals, dieting to avoid "fatness" and its sequelae is a way to disidentify with femininity and its inferior, powerless, unattractive, and insecure status in society. The disavowal of femininity in the families of eating-disordered individuals is also prevalent, and often can be identified in attitudes and behavior apart from the symptomatic, eating-disordered individual.

> Carol, a bulimic 28-year-old woman, entered therapy with her fiancé because she and her partner were having difficulty deciding about whether or not to get married. Both of her parents were constantly exercising and dieting in order to be fit and trim. Her mother had a terrible relationship with Carol's maternal grandmother, and both women admired Carol's narcissistically withdrawn father, "who knew what life was about." Carol was encouraged to go into business or law, which were "really in the man's world," as "a woman's life is a drag." Carol's mother suffered from chronic depressions and fragile self-esteem. She, too, may have had BN.

Root et al. (1986), who work from a systemic, feminist orientation, suggest that this disidentification is a self-destructive attempt to escape from the perceived helplessness and powerlessness of the woman's world to what society views as the powerful, secure man's world. Woodman

(1982), a Jungian analytic therapist, proposes that the eating disorders can be conceptualized at an individual level as part of a struggle against a negative feminine/maternal identification, which is held at bay through the use of the masculine world's focus on ideals, perfection, and control. The eating disorder functions to keep the female child from transforming into a woman by remaining boyish or functioning like a man. This prevents the inevitable "loss" of the child to the family through the route of her normal sexual maturation and is consonant with the family's identification with socially acceptable masculine traits. Thus, the eating disorder, a form of dietary androgyny, solves the two major concerns faced by the insecure family system: the issues of social acceptance and loss of a family member.

Regardless of theoretical orientation, all observers concur about the sensitivity of the eating-disordered family to social values that are experienced as external to the family, whether they be the values of a specific ethnic group or of society at large. This sensitivity has been commented on by Fossum and Mason (1986) as an example of shame-bound functioning within family systems. The ideals and values used by these families to diminish their shame (or sensitivity) and increase the sense of security are traditionally associated with masculine stereotypes; for example, performance, competence, and achievement. This pursuit helps the family find a secure link to its social context, which is experienced as valuing the masculine world of work and competition and devaluing femininity, and thus stabilizes the family's sense of connectedness. The resulting sense of security provides the family with a way of dealing with its unresolved history of loss and isolation. By subscribing fully to external social values, the family feels as if it rightfully belongs. It has paid the price of admission. The shame of social disconnection and isolation is, therefore, partially averted as long as everyone is doing the socially correct thing and subscribes to the values that the family's social context currently holds as central. In the case of an eating-disordered individual's family, perfectionism, competitiveness, and achievement are often key social values. At an individual level, the eating-disordered individual is bound to her family of origin through

her dietary androgyny, which diverts her from seeking sexually motivated peer group relationship.

The eating-disordered individual's role in helping her family of origin to maintain its adaptation requires two major contributions that are
at the center of her conflict: remaining engaged in the system and
embodying family values even if they are destructive to the self. This
may thwart the possibility of marriage for some individuals, but when
it does not, the individual must still retain a crucial stabilizing role in
the family of origin regardless of the consequences for the marital relationship.

THE MARITAL DILEMMAS

Marriage and the Family Legacy

When eating-disordered offspring marry, their families face a possible need to restructure. This provides both an element of hope and one
of danger: hope that somehow the union will provide an infusion of the
security and resources for the family, and danger that the newcomer will
expose the shame and dysfunction of the family of origin. The ambivalence of eating-disordered families can be seen even during the dating
process. They tend to be either overly inclusive of their child's prospec-
tive mate or they are distant and aloof. As a father of a bulimic daughter
states: "We feel that our daughter's boyfriends are *our* friends and we
should get close to them."

The eating disordered individual's hope that the spouse will provide
such resources as security, affirmation, and acceptance for her family is
often complemented by the partner's expectation that the marital relationship will be secured by providing these resources for his in-laws.
The task of building a marital partnership quickly becomes secondary
to the role of stabilizing the patient's family of origin, and the eating-
disordered individual and her partner become involved in "parenting"
the family of origin.

Andrew, a bulimic's husband, felt that they ought to spend all
their weekend and holiday time with his wife's parents because
"they were such nice people and were so considerate." His bulimic
wife thought that this was marvelous until she began to realize
how much bingeing and vomiting she did after she spent any time
with her parents.

If the eating disorder began before marriage, the "healthy spouse"
usually enters into the marriage aware of the day-to-day problems created by the illness and of the extent of his partner's family overinvolvement and insecurity. In this situation, the healthy spouse is often
focused on securing his own position in the relationship through care
giving, and he substitutes the closeness of the care-giving process for
true intimacy. Given this scenario, the eating disorder can actually stabilize the relationship and create a codependency. The husband, then,
may actually be worried about his wife's changing, afraid that she will
not be interested in him when she becomes healthy.

When the eating disorder appears after some years of marriage, the
spouse often experiences guilt and shame about somehow "causing"
the eating problem. He may become overly involved in caring for his
spouse and fixing it; which might be called the dynamic of repair.
He may feel angry and betrayed and distance himself from the
afflicted partner, thereby setting up a dynamic of denial. The
dynamic of repair suggests an anxious insecure attachment pattern,
and the dynamic of denial an avoidant insecure attachment pattern.
Both dynamics are maintained by the spouse's perception of his role
in the illness and prevent him from functioning as a partner in the
marriage. In the first instance, he becomes a parent, whereas in the
second, he threatens separation.

The eating-disordered partner is also impaired in dealing with the
marital situation because her focus is so often directed toward her family of origin and not the marriage. She is required to develop a trusting,
secure marital relationship, although she has no history of secure relationships. This is an impossible bind: having to succeed in a relation-

ship without having the basic relational tools. Small wonder that the eating-disordered individual often uses secrecy and lying to hide both the illness and the relational inadequacies. No matter what is missing, the patient is dedicated to "protecting the family of origin's cover." Going for or accepting help is always difficult because it indicates publicly that a member of a perfect family is imperfect, and this threatens the patient's ability to control external perceptions, which in the past has functioned as a substitute for growth and development.

The following case study helps illustrate the intergenerational and internal tensions in the eating-disordered system where sexuality, marriage, and generativity are sacrificed to maintaining a secure base and avoiding shame.

Alice, a 24-year-old woman with AN, had been married for about a year when she was admitted to the Day Hospital Program (DHP). She was the oldest in a family of three children, and the first to marry. Her mother had grown up in a cool, distant family, and had deliberately married into Alice's father's large, cohesive, and ethnically distinct family to derive a sense of belonging that she had not experienced in her own family of origin. Alice's father was attracted to his wife largely because of her apparent compliance with the expectations of his own cultural milieu.

Alice continued to live at home throughout her college years and during her initial employment. She had an extremely close relationship with her mother, which seemed to play a role in stabilizing the parents' marriage, a union that had become somewhat distant. Alice's mother was concerned about both her own weight and Alice's weight. They often dieted in tandem.

Alice met her husband-to-be at the gym, and the couple quickly established an exclusive relationship, including a mutually satisfying sexual relationship. She was attracted to her husband's coolness and intellectuality. In this regard, he resembled Alice's maternal grandmother. The husband was attracted to the idea that Alice would take care of him (a quality that he observed in both Alice and her mother) and make up for the nurturance he did not receive in his family.

Alice began to diet rigidly and to vomit the day after she became engaged. She continued to lose weight, and a few months before the wedding, she discontinued all sexual contact with her partner, telling him that she wished to become a "born again virgin."

Her fiancé's grandmother, who lived in the same community as Alice's parents, died shortly before the couple were to be married. Her fiancé's parents offered the couple the use of the grandmother's house; and he accepted on Alice's and his behalf. Although this decision enraged Alice, as she had hoped to live in her parents' home after the marriage, she was too ill to protest.

Alice's weight reached its lowest point on her wedding day, and her family took her to the hospital because she was in severe abdominal pain as a result of constipation of two months' duration. However, her parents did not see her emaciation as a major problem at this time.

The couple did not consummate the marriage and had not done so by the time Alice came to treatment one year later, even though they were living together in the husband's grandmother's house. During treatment, Alice drew pictures of this house, describing it as having a "horrible eerie quality." As she began to gain weight, she became contemptuous of her husband. The alliance between her husband and her mother, which was centered around their concerns about her debilitated physical state, evaporated. By the time she was discharged, her plan was to leave her husband and return home to her mother.

The Struggle for Security: Relational Power and Control

The struggle for security in the eating-disordered marital relationship is often hidden and is expressed as a struggle for power and control. Power issues are often part of a couple's concerns and reflect the identification with the currently valued ideal of being in charge of one's life. Power and control are also chosen because they offer the possibility of inducing (displacing onto) shame in the partner, and at the same time represent more highly valued masculine stereotypes. When the underlying issue of trust and security is broached in treatment, the power struggle usually dissipates.

Boundary issues in the relationship are also problematic. Just as in the family of origin, the marital duo struggles for security so that both overinvolvement (protest phase behavior) and distancing (avoidant phase behavior) are quite common.

> In order to "help" his bulimic wife, Elaine, Bob was punctilious in stocking exactly the correct type and amount of soda that Elaine used to induce vomiting. He drove her to clinics for Demerol shots and spent hours talking to her in order "to understand and be close to her." He felt that her marriage to him left her unfulfilled and that he had to "look after her disappointment." He was uncomfortable about giving up this role because he would feel helpless and excluded from her life. Elaine considered his help very important, and found the therapist's suggestion that she look after her own vomiting unhelpful.

When the eating-disordered partner has a history of physical or sexual abuse, there is enormous amplification of the issues around control and boundary, as well as around the hidden agenda of lack of security and trust.

Gender and Sexuality

Gender issues are another problem as the couple attempts to develop a sexual relationship together. The eating disorder may protect the couple from an awareness of their respective conflicts in these areas. Feminine identification is particularly difficult for the eating-disordered woman, and the man in this marriage may himself be frightened of closeness with a "real woman." The patient's androgynous tendencies are somewhat relieving for her "woman-shy" spouse. As a result, sexuality for the couple is compromised.

Charles, the spouse of a bulimic woman, was concerned about the possibility that he might be a homosexual. He felt that this in part explained her anorgasmic state during intercourse, but "did not want to deal with these issues because they were too upsetting."

Bob, another spouse of an anorexic woman who later became bulimic, was worried about his sexual potency and was satisfied with no sexual relationship. His wife was not upset with this state of affairs.

Many bulimic people have a history of sexual abuse. The sexual dysfunction that results from this experience is often crippling for the individual (Gelinas, 1983), and consequently for the couple. The sexual dysfunction, which can include diminished sexual drive, body-image distortions, and flashbacks related to sexual activity and difficulties with orgasm, requires specific treatment separate from that of the eating disorder. However, success in treating the eating disorder and normalization of eating can lead to an increased awareness of the sexual dysfunction once the disorder no longer serves as a means of regulating concerns about one's physical self and intimacy.

Two patients, Diane and Freda, both had BN, and they both had experienced severe, prolonged sexual abuse as children. They were perceived by their husbands as extremely sexually desirable, and had engaged in intense sexual activity for brief periods early in their relationships. However, both women experienced a total lack of sexual drive as a result of the sexual abuse and were extremely frightened about being touched. Although the husbands expected that an increase in sexual drive would accompany normalization of eating, the reverse occurred: Diane and Freda became increasingly dissatisfied with their bodies as they began to recover more memories of having been abused.

Intergenerational Pushes and Pulls

The intergenerational transmission of an insecure attachment style puts the newly formed couple in an impossible situation. Their families of origin did not provide them with the tools and security with which to create a marital relationship, while at the same time, they expect the couple to "do well in the marriage." In addition, the couple know that they must succeed to ensure that their families will avoid shame and feel secure and worthwhile. As a result, the couple will be forced to turn inwards into the marital relationship and look only to each other and to their children to provide what is missing. This load is simply too heavy to bear, leading to the parentification of children (see Chapter 8) and overwhelming stress in the marital relationship.

SUMMARY

This chapter provided a framework for understanding the eating-disordered marriage by exploring family-of-origin dynamics in families with eating-disordered members. This exploration led to a formulation of the central issues in the eating-disordered marriage, which focused on the role of attachment and shame. Finally, certain issues that are of importance in the treatment of the eating-disordered marriage were highlighted by the use of case examples.

4

Assessment of
the Couple

This chapter presents an assessment format that assumes that the assessing therapist is aware that one or both members of the couple suffers from an eating disorder. Routine assessment of couple functioning/ dysfunctioning may not reveal this fact unless the therapist asks about it specifically or one member of the couple is obviously emaciated. Any undetected conditions, including eating disorders, are likely to have an adverse effect on the course of marital treatment. As marital therapists begin routinely to inquire about sexual and physical abuse, they may also benefit from a brief evaluation of eating habits and concerns about body image when assessing couples.

STAGES OF THE ASSESSMENT

The assessment is comprised of several parts, most of which are similar to a standard basic marital assessment, including an individual, family-of-origin, and couple history, as well as an evaluation of the couple's problem-solving strengths and weaknesses (Table 4.1). One area that is perhaps unique in this assessment is the focus on the couple's eating and exercise patterns and the importance of appearance and shape in the relationship. We believe that this information is profoundly important in couples where one member is suffering from an eating disorder, as

Table 4.1.
Stages of the Marital Assessment

Reason for the assessment
Understanding of the eating disorder
Couple History
Sexual history
Individual histories
Role of food, exercise, and appearance in the marriage
Problem-solving abilities

it provides the basis for dealing with the acute need for normalizing eating and the longer-term goal of developing a more accepting stance toward weight and shape.

Context of the Assessment

The assessment may vary slightly, depending on the context of the referral; that is, whether it is part of an intensive treatment program, or whether a physician, psychiatrist, or other source has referred the couple for treatment to a therapist in private practice. In the latter situation, we see it as optimal for the eating-disordered partner to remain under medical supervision or treatment during the course of marital treatment, as couple therapy by itself is not likely to be sufficient for the behavioral symptoms of the eating disorder. This is in keeping with the multidimensional approach to treatment (Garfinkel & Garner, 1982) discussed in Chapter 1.

If the couple has been self-referred, it will be important to refer the spouse with the eating disorder to a physician, who will monitor the patient's medical condition and possibly assist in coordinating efforts to obtain treatment for eating symptoms. It is also necessary that the physician and marital therapist discuss the patient's minimum weight and arrangements regarding hospitalization. We suggest that these arrangements be explicit and overt; in other words, discussed with the couple openly and made an integral part of the treatment contract.

Whether this is done with both the marital therapist and the physician present will depend on the situation; those therapists fortunate enough to have developed a good liaison with a number of physicians will likely be able to depend on these physicians to manage the patient's physical symptoms in a manner consistent with the therapist's approach. When a new liaison is being established, it may be advisable for the therapist to have a preliminary meeting with the physician to discuss approaches and goals, and a joint meeting with the couple at which the responsibility for different aspects of the couple's care is clearly delineated. The development of therapist-physician liaisons is time consuming, but it is ultimately worthwhile.

If the patient is engaged in a treatment program, couple therapy may be one of numerous treatment modalities. In this situation, the therapist will already have access to much information about the patient and the background of her eating disorder. The marital therapist will also be assured that the patient has other avenues to help her deal with her behavioral symptoms, sexual concerns, feelings of low self-esteem, and the plethora of other issues that are part of a comprehensive treatment of an eating disorder. For example, in our setting at the Eating Disorder Day Hospital Program (DHP) at The Toronto Hospital, married patients are involved in couple and family therapy and in many groups, including ones that focus on food- and non–food-related issues, such as body image, sexuality, and family relations (Piran & Kaplan, 1990; Shekter-Wolfson & Woodside, 1991).

Reason for the Assessment

Why have the couple sought out marital treatment? Who is the driving force behind the marital treatment?

In this part of the assessment, the focus is on how the couple understand their decision to attend a marital treatment. Questions focus on the process by which the decision was made and how power and control issues have entered into this decision. Patients involved in an intensive treatment program for an eating disorder will have different reasons to engage in marital work than patients not separately engaged in treatment for an eating disorder. For example, a patient with AN may be motivated to come for marital treatment only to reduce conflict within the relationship, but she may have no desire to deal with her AN, as it has become ego-enhancing rather than ego-dystonic. Some patients with BN may be motivated to seek treatment to terminate a relationship while wishing to deal with their bingeing and vomiting behavior. These two scenarios are represented in the following case examples.

Grace, age 27, was admitted to the Day Hospital suffering from AN of seven years duration and recurrent psychotic depressions. She was enormously ambivalent about the behavioral component of the program, but was eager to stabilize her marriage, fearing that she would not be given custody of their only child if the marriage were to break up.

Helen, age 32, was married for the second time and had three children. She had a 17-year history of AN and BN. She presented as distraught about her eating symptoms, but stated clearly during her assessment that she had mixed feelings about remaining in her marriage and planned to review this once her eating was more stable.

In some cases, the spouse or couple may not be clear as to why they have been referred for marital therapy. They may question what the marriage has to do with the eating disorder or the reverse. In these situations, the therapist may need to help the couple focus on the effects of the BN or AN on the marriage, rather than look at factors in the marriage that may have initiated or perpetuated the problem. The therapist can encourage this shift in focus with open, supportive statements such as: "When someone in a relationship is sick, I know that everyone close to that person will be experiencing all sorts of difficult feelings such as anger, frustration, guilt, and helplessness. I also know that the person who is sick is often feeling the same way. Unfortunately, these feelings are rarely addressed except under stress or when there is a crisis."

By addressing the couple this way, issues of blame and shame are minimized. However, the issue of blame should be carefully and openly addressed, particularly if the eating disorder became more symptomatic or was disclosed after the marriage. When this is the case, the spouse may feel that "my wife was well until I married her." This type of feeling will likely lead to an activation of the attachment system (described in Chapter 3), which must be carefully monitored.

Ed was not aware that his wife, Irene, had an eating disorder. Irene had led him to believe that she was seeing a stomach specialist for her weight loss, and she told Ed that the specialist had asked her to bring him to an appointment. On the way to the interview, she informed him that she was actually being assessed for the Day Hospital Program. Naturally, he went into a state of shock. He needed the assessment time to ask questions about the problem, to help him deal with his anger about not having been told about the problem, and to cope with his guilt for not having noticed himself.

There may be disagreements as to who views marital issues as more significant. When the referral is from the patient's physician or therapist, this may set up a situation in which the spouse feels left out of what he perceives to be a physician–patient coalition.

Jill, a 32-year-old woman, had been married for five years and had one daughter. She had suffered from AN and BN for many years. Engaged in individual therapy for about a year prior to hospitalization, she had concluded that her husband was to blame for her ongoing eating symptoms, and had convinced her therapist of this as well. The therapist's referral reflected this view. While the therapist acknowledged the existence of marital problems, he did not see those problems as relevant to her eating.

Occasionally, referrals are made for treatment by family physicians or therapists who are responding to spousal anxiety about the patient's physical condition, which tends to result in the patient feeling as if she has been ganged up on by her husband and the referring therapist. In cases in which the spouse is not entirely aware of the extent of the eating symptomatology and the patient wishes to maintain this secrecy, the referring individual may be told "everything is fine at home" as a way of attempting further to separate marital issues from eating issues. This may produce a coalition of the couple against helping professionals.

The second and third situations described above are exemplified by Kathy.

Kathy's physician was fully aware of her symptoms, her spouse and parents less so. She was admitted twice to the DHP. During the first admission, she acknowledged the severity of her symptoms to her physician, to whom she minimized her marital discord, which included an open extramarital affair on her part. By the time of her second admission, she was minimizing her eating symptoms to her parents and husband, who were all much more concerned about her deteriorating marriage.

Couple's Understanding of the Eating Disorder

What does the spouse understand about the illness? How did he find out? Had he suspected before he found out? What does he think causes this type of illness? How does he think these factors apply to his spouse?

This section focuses on developing an understanding of how much the spouse knows and understands about the nature of the illness. If the identified patient is clearly anorexic, she is likely to have a different understanding or personal experience of her marriage than would a covert or secretive bulimic whose partner recently discovered her problem. When the patient looks outwardly "normal" and appears to have been functioning well, it may be particularly difficult for the spouse.

Although there may have been clues such as candy wrappers, open food packages, traces of vomit in the toilet, or frequent visits to the washroom, these usually are overlooked, consciously or unconsciously.

> Fred's wife discovered his large restaurant bills on her credit card statement. Although the bills had initially been explained as business expenses, she became suspicious. When Fred's bulimia was finally acknowledged, she was confused. She first blamed herself, but was later extremely angry at her husband for lying, even though he had left clues.

Fred's wife needed some information about bulimia, not only regarding physical complications, but also about the psychological issues that are often seen; for example, some patients are so ashamed of their behavior and are so out of control that they try to conceal it. This often includes lying.

An AN patient's physical condition is much more obvious, as she is emaciated and is unable to eat. In these cases, the spouse may describe feelings of frustration, not understanding why the patient claims that she still has weight to lose and cannot see the need to gain weight. Here, the therapist will need to focus early on giving the couple some basic information about eating disorders.

Couple History

How did they meet? What was the initial attraction? (Did this include a focus on appearance, weight, or shape?) How did they decide to establish an exclusive relationship? How did they decide to get married?

The couple history should include not only how the couple met and how the relationship proceeded, but also specifically what it was about the other person that was attractive. This information is very important, as looks, weight, or shape may have been key factors in what attracted the individuals to each other, and it will naturally have implications for treatment. The weight gain that usually accompanies treatment for both AN and BN may mean changing the appearance that the spouse initially found attractive. The spouse may covertly oppose the need for maintenance of a normal weight, which would affect appearance, and he may harbor the hope that the patient can still recover by focusing solely on nonfood issues. Other factors related to the eating disorder may also play a role in the initial attraction. Van den Broucke and Vandereycken (1989b) suggest that if the partner was anorexic before the couple met, it could be assumed that "the existence of the eating disorder is crucial to the stability of the relationship."

Fred (described earlier) developed his eating disorder while in high school. He was a star athlete, but tended to gain weight easily. He developed a pattern of chronic dieting that helped him maintain a weight appropriate for his athletic activities, but eventually led to both AN and BN. He met his wife in high school at what he called his "good weight." They got married just before graduation, because she became pregnant. Fred kept his eating disorder a secret from his wife for many years. He sought work in another city, which meant that he had to be out of the house before breakfast and would not return until after dinner. This arrangement permitted him to binge both on his way to work and on his way home. When the illness got to the point that he no longer could work, he decided to seek help. After his wife questioned his behavior and discovered the illness, he found himself more accountable to her both financially and physically. The marriage, which had existed calmly at a distance for several years, became conflictual and they were close to separation when they finally came for marital treatment.

Louise was a very attractive, tall, thin cheerleader in the high school where her husband was a football star. The couple married soon after graduation. Louise had always been a dieter during her teenage years, but maintained a fairly stable and normal weight. After the marriage, her weight began to drop, and later, after the birth of her children, she attempted to lose more weight, as she felt that her husband only found her attractive when she was quite thin. Several nights a week, she worked as a bar pianist and had to wear costumes that required her to remain slender. For the most part, however, her eating disorder kept her at home, as she did not feel very confident getting a job or going out during the day. In individual treatment, she began to feel more confident, and she said that she wanted to quit her evening job and find another type of job that would get her out during the day.

Although, in this case, the husband had not openly been aware of his wife's eating disorder, he implied that he liked his wife at home because she was more available to him and to the children. In the course of her recovery, the previous balance in the relationship was seriously disrupted, causing significant distress for the husband.

The issue of the eating disorder being crucial to marital stability is not seen in all situations.

One couple came for therapy before marriage for fear that the eating disorder would impair their relationship. Both members of the couple felt that the eating disorder needed to be controlled before they could make any definite decisions about a long-term commitment. While the patient was engaged in separate treatment for her eating symptoms, the couple worked on issues such as problem solving, sexual concerns, relationships with friends and family, his role in her eating, and their fears of being committed to each other. The couple was seen for one year and did eventually marry.

Some patients do not develop their eating disorder until after marriage, and the dynamics of this situation seem to be unique. The onset of the eating disorder may occur after a significant life event such as the birth of a child or a crisis such as marital stress or professional pressure. When AN develops after the marriage, it may represent a recurrence of an episode that had taken place before the marriage (Andersen, 1985), or it may be rooted in unresolved developmental conflicts (Van den Broucke & Vandereycken, 1989b; Dally, 1984).

Mary, age 34, had developed AN at age 32 in the context of a deteriorating marital situation. While she had been a chronic dieter for many years and a gymnast in her teens, she had not developed a full-blown eating disorder until her marriage began to disintegrate.

Kathy (described earlier) had experienced an episode of AN during her teenage years, which had resolved around the time she became engaged; the episode that brought her to treatment represented a relapse after several years' remission.

Sexual History

When did the couple become sexually active? Who initiated this? How do the couple feel currently about their sexual relationship? What specific areas of problems exist? Are there areas of difficulty related specifically to the eating disorder?

The marital history must also encompass an understanding of the couple's sexual history, including a detailed history of the couple's sexual life, from the perspective of both partners. It is not unusual to hear about difficulties with sexual activity, which are exacerbated by the eating disorder. The patient who does not feel good about the way she looks physically is likely to have difficulty feeling sexually attractive. In some cases, the couple have not had a sexual relationship for years (Russell, 1979).

Alice (described in Chapter 3) met her husband at the gym and they initiated a mutually satisfactory sexual life. All went well until their engagement was announced, when the patient, who had significant conflicts in the area of autonomy, began to lose weight and vomit. The decrease in the frequency of sexual intercourse paralleled the patient's weight, which reached its nadir on their wedding day. The couple had been married a year when she came to treatment; they had not yet consummated the marriage.

The couple may also have a great deal of difficulty discussing sex with a therapist. It is important to assure the couple that feelings of embarrassment are quite normal.

The couple might be asked questions that include: Do you have a sexual relationship? What aspects do you find most enjoyable? What aspects do you find least enjoyable? In addition, the therapist should gather a detailed history of their earlier sexual relationship, including their initial sexual experiences. The therapist should note whether there has been a shift in the level of sexual satisfaction before and after the onset of the eating disorder, and since marriage or moving in together. As mentioned before, the patient may have always had an eating disorder, though it was not known at the time. It is always useful to assess subjective differences in sexual satisfaction before and after the spouse became aware of the eating disorder.

Helen (described earlier) and her husband noted that their sexual life had been very active in the initial stages of their courtship, with Helen being very aggressive sexually. After disclosing her eating disorder to her husband and deciding to seek treatment, she described herself as "feeling repelled" and uninterested in sexual activity.

Some patients feel very responsible for the couple's poor sexual relationship.

Harold had been an alcoholic before he developed AN. In his earlier years of marriage, he found he was able to arouse his wife even though he was drinking heavily. However, as time went on and he developed AN, he became impotent and withdrew completely from the couple's sexual life. He felt ashamed and angry at himself.

Some patients may be experiencing sexual abuse in their marriage. The therapist should specifically ask the couple about ongoing physical or sexual abuse. The couple may not readily talk about the problem during the assessment, especially if they have developed a shame-bound system as described in Chapter 3. A related problem arises when sexual activity in the marriage becomes a continuous reminder of one partner's sexually abusive experiences in the past, and thus becomes compromised within the marriage.

Diane and Freda (described earlier) were members of the Day Hospital at the same time. Both openly spoke of the sexual difficulties in their marriage, but attributed their own absent sexual drive to their chronic dissatisfaction with their bodies; that is, they were frightened of being touched, and felt so fat that they could not imagine their husbands to be interested in them sexually. Only when Diane, and then Freda, disclosed their histories of incestuous sexual abuse did they also acknowledge experiencing flashbacks of earlier abuse during sexual activity in their marriage.

If it is known that physical or sexual abuse is taking place, the therapist will need to make the physical safety of each member of the couple an urgent priority—whether by advising the couple to live separately or by some other means. We believe that other therapeutic work cannot proceed in the face of ongoing abuse, and that it is essential that abuse be explicitly labeled as such.

Individual Histories

What are the significant life events for each member of the couple? Has either member experienced significant violations of boundaries?

Boundary Issues—Marital/Interpersonal

In this part of the interview, it is important to explore the history of interaction in the couple's families of origin, and to detail the current ongoing relationships between the couples and their families in order to assess the level of individuation from the family of origin (Bowen, 1978). This is useful for treatment planning because the degree of differentiation of self largely depends on the course of one's family history, which is often repeated in the current nuclear family (Nichols, 1984). In interviewing some couples, therapists will be told that the couple have very little to do with their own families, and this pattern is viewed as being indicative of having achieved a separation, when, in fact, physical separation may be masking a more profound problem with differentiation and autonomy. Dysfunctional relational patterns established in families of origin may appear to haunt the couple as these patterns unexpectedly recur. An understanding of each member's family of origin is a critical tool in understanding dysfunction in the current marriage.

Boundary Issues—Sexual abuse

Assessing experiences of sexual abuse on the part of both partners is particularly important in this population, as noted in Chapters 2 and 3. Sexual abuse as a child may not be revealed unless it is specifically elicited. For example, it might be useful to ask: "It is not uncommon for people who have eating disorders to have been sexually abused. Have you ever been touched in a way that you felt uncomfortable with or that was painful either as a child or as an adult?"

In some cases, the information gathered may be new to the other partner, and result in mixed feelings, including anger and disgust.

Simply asking these types of questions will not always result in a disclosure; it may, however, allow the abused member of the couple to feel as if he or she has permission to talk about these issues on another occasion.

Harold (described earlier) eventually disclosed his own childhood sexual abuse by a family friend to a group in the Day Hospital after several other members talked about their own experiences. The group supported him and his decision to inform both his wife and his parents about the abuse. The family response was positive, and each member was able to explain how this information clarified some of Harold's previous behavior, which had not been understood.

Therapists must be prepared for the distress that accompanies both the recognition of abuse and its reporting. The active reliving of the trauma in the form of flashbacks may cause the patient to engage in various forms of self-destructive behaviors as a way to distract attention from the memories. This type of reaction is the norm, and it always affects the pace and focus of whatever therapy or assessment is occurring.

Intergenerational Boundaries

What have been the significant events in each partner's family of origin? How has each family dealt with issues of loss and change? In addition to sexual and boundary issues, the therapist must also detail how the respective families of origin have dealt with and adapted to various family-life-cycle events such as losses and significant changes.

Nancy, a 25-year-old bulimic/anorexic woman, suffered numerous losses while growing up, including the separation of her parents. As a result, she felt that if she stayed in her marriage, she would continue to experience losses as she had as an adolescent. Nancy had never had an opportunity to discuss these fears with anyone, nor did she volunteer the information unless specifically asked. She felt a great deal of shame over her parents' separation and felt the same shame when thinking about failing in her current relationship.

At times, boundary weakness between generations is manifested by behavior on the part of the family of origin, which actively interferes with the couple's ability to focus on their own development.

Opal's mother continued to bring meals to her married daughter on the weekends. By the time Opal was admitted to a treatment program, her mother was feeding her every day. The therapist's task was to help the mother give up the meal preparation without feeling hurt or too abandoned, while working with the couple to take over this daily task.

Genograms

Genograms can be a helpful tool in getting a good working summary of a couple's families of origin. Such issues as life-cycle events, quality of relationships, and illnesses can be highlighted (McGoldrick & Gerson, 1985).

A genogram is a concrete, tangible picture of the family that can easily be amended as new information is revealed. McGoldrick and Gerson (1985) use the genogram as an efficient tool to summarize and present information to families. They also suggest that genograms can help the therapist to join with the family, clarify family patterns, reframe issues, and detoxify family conflicts. They point out that a three-generation genogram is most suited for families or couples presenting for treatment, as such a genogram reframes the couple or family in a larger context where significant life events, losses, and relationship qualities can be appreciated.

Figure 4.1 illustrates the following case.

A Family Genogram

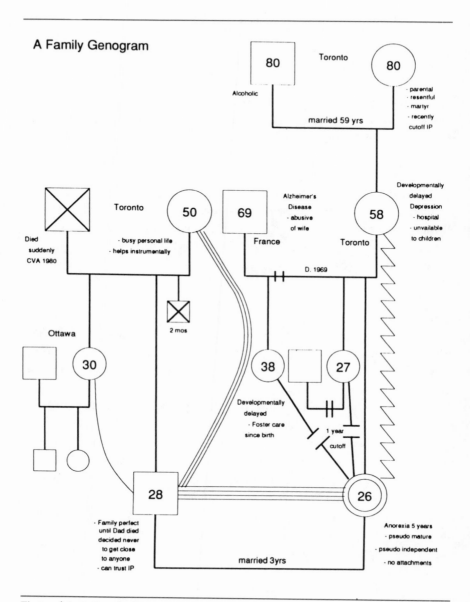

Figure 4.1. A Sample Genogram

Pam, age 26, has suffered from AN for five years and has been married for three years. Her husband openly expressed his fear of becoming intimate, ascribing this to the pain he experienced when his father died, an event that made him decide that the pain of loss outweighed the joy of attachments. Pam had been raised largely by her grandmother, as her own mother was frequently unable to perform her parenting role because of a serious psychiatric illness that necessitated a lengthy stay at a hospital. In addition, the mother had been diagnosed as developmentally delayed. Pam's parents' marriage was marked by physical abuse. Of Pam's siblings, one sister, also developmentally delayed, was made a permanent ward of the province after the local Children's Aid became involved. Her other sister had been involved in a very stressful relationship that had ended in a complete cutoff one year prior to Pam's couple assessment. The multiple losses, abuse, and psychiatric morbidity in the family appeared to contribute to Pam's development of a pseudomature and hypervigilant relationship style, and ultimately to her developing AN as a coping mechanism for her own and her family's distress.

Role of Food, Exercise, and Appearance in a Relationship

How often do the partners eat together? Where do they eat? Who is responsible for shopping and cooking? How are these decisions made? What food preferences does each member of the couple have? How much does each partner exercise? What does each member of the couple think about his or her own and the partner's weight and shape?

As mentioned earlier, issues around food and appearance are particularly relevant in a relationship when one member of the couple has an eating disorder. As appearance is central to maintaining a relationship, and changes in appearance related to weight gain may actually threaten it, it is important to explore the exact role that food and exercise play.

As part of the assessment of the role of food for the couple, it is helpful to understand the role it plays in each member's family of origin. The therapist needs to ask specific questions, including how the partners spend time together, how they spend time around mealtime, who cooks the meals, how often they get together for meals, and whether or not they can eat together comfortably. If the eating disorder has always been part of the marriage, it is likely that the couple will not have developed a strategy to deal with mealtimes. However, if the eating disorder has been acknowledged later, a strategy may have been developed, albeit an unhelpful one.

Querida, a 30-year-old woman with BN, had binged her way up to a comparatively high weight within two years of her marriage. Both she and her husband were aware of her need to eat more normally to stop the bingeing: in an effort to help her, her husband continually reminded her that she "could always lose the weight later on." Querida felt his reminders made her more aware of her eating patterns, which in turn exacerbated her bingeing.

Specific questions about the couple's exercise and activity level are also important.

Rhona had met her husband at a fitness club and the couple spent most of their leisure time together there. However, after Rhona entered the Day Hospital, she found that the time requirements of the fitness program conflicted with her treatment. In addition, she was prohibited from exercising as it represented a form of purging for her. Rhona was understandably concerned that these issues would have a direct impact on her marriage, especially as her self-esteem was low enough that she believed that it was only her physical appearance that kept him in the relationship. Her husband was very upset at the prohibition against exercising as he felt that this type of activity was helpful in increasing her self-esteem: he also acknowledged being attracted to a specific body shape. Rhona was also concerned that he might begin to develop interests that did not involve her—which did, in fact, occur.

The therapist eventually negotiated limited exercise in the form of recreational cycling as a nonpurgative form of physical activity that allowed them to continue their shared interest.

Another important question will include how pleased or disappointed the partner is with the patient's current shape, and his fears, if any, about his spouse's potential change in shape. Although the fear of change may be more of an issue for the patient than for the spouse, the patient may still worry that the spouse will become disappointed and abandon her.

> Fred (described above) was tremendously afraid that weight gain would adversely affect his relationship with his wife. His shape was also tied in to his feelings of aging, and he was very proud that people often mistook his daughter for his wife. On the other hand, his wife did not seem to find her husband's shape and possible weight gain as much of a problem as he did. The couple had met in high school, where he had been very active in sports, and his sense of self-worth was closely identified with his athletic accomplishments. Shape and physique were important to him before the eating disorder, and continued to be so in his marriage.

Problem-Solving Abilities

What problems have the couple had to face in their marriage? How have they tried to solve these problems? What are the biggest unsolved problems in their marriage?

This part of the assessment examines the couple's problem-solving abilities. The therapist should seek examples of attempts at conflict resolution by exploring how the couple resolves current problems related to the eating disorder and to all aspects of their everyday relationship.

More than likely, many attempts have been made to solve problems related to the eating disorder, especially if it has been long-standing or is distressing to one or both members of the couple. Evaluation of their problem-solving ability will help to assess how rigid or flexible the couple is: Can they discuss relevant marital issues, such as the household budget, child rearing, housing, and social activities, or are they focused on the current physical state of the patient? The information will help the therapist to define the couple's strengths and weaknesses. This part of the assessment has a focus similar to that of Foster (1986) in that it seeks to assess the couple's ability to reformulate the symptoms as relational difficulties.

> Susan was living with her ex-fiancé. In the couple assessment, her boyfriend had a great deal of difficulty not focusing on the topic of her eating disorder. Even though she was involved in an intensive program, he felt he was the only one who understood her problem. The couple had broken off a previous engagement, but when the therapist attempted to ask the couple about the engagement, the boyfriend deflected the questions and returned to the eating problem.

Often, spouses view the illness in relatively unsophisticated ways.

> Querida's husband (described previously) responded to her fear of further weight gain by encouraging her not to eat the high-calorie food provided for her in her meal plan; this advice persisted despite efforts by the therapist to explain the connections between dietary restriction and bingeing.

SPECIAL ISSUES

Meal Sessions as an Assessment Technique

Some therapists eat with the family during the assessment in order to see how the issue of food is viewed by the family, but we do not routinely include this in our initial assessment. We occasionally use a meal in the first or second session postassessment, not to externalize potential conflict as in a Minuchin-like family meal (Minuchin et al., 1978, p. 120), but to assess boundary issues, such as who regulates eating in the couple.

The meal session can also be part of the treatment process, and is further described in Chapter 5.

Assessment Tools

As part of the assessment, there are some objective tools that may be used to assist both the couple and the therapist. Psychometric measures of family functioning can aid the therapist in a number of ways. First, the results can provide the therapist with information about conflicts or areas of strength not previously assessed, which can then help to avoid therapist bias or blindness. Second, systems language and concepts are often confusing for families: seeing a visual depiction of family functioning can help families focus attention on important issues. These measures may be particularly important for couples who are loath to describe differences while in session, or for couples who are normally exclusively fixated on physical symptoms. We use the Family Assessment Measurement (FAM) (Skinner, Steinhauer, & Santa-Barbara, 1983) and the Waring Intimacy Questionnaire (WIQ) (Waring & Reddon, 1983), which are described in detail in Chapter 7. These assessment tools should be used as an adjunct to the material that is collected through the clinical interview. The tools can also be useful for couples having difficulty in identifying concerns outside of the eating disorder.

The FAM and WIQ were very useful with one older couple who were highly educated and articulate. The husband, in particular, could talk very knowledgably about his wife's problem. It was evident that he had done a great deal of reading. However, he was unable to conceptualize or discuss problems with marital communication, or the expression of feelings or values. The FAM results showed discrepant features in the above three areas. His scores were in the average range, whereas his wife's scores were elevated somewhat into the problem range. She noted that she had often felt differently than her husband did, but rarely expressed disagreement. It was not so much the actual areas of discrepancy that were important, but the fact that the scores were different. "Difference" became an important theme for this couple as therapy progressed. The WIQs showed differences in the area of sexuality, which was a useful starting point for the discussion concerning the couple's sexual relationship.

Couples with Children

The assessment should ask about any children the couple have. Most often the patient is responsible for the children, making this part of the assessment very important. The parents' views regarding their children's eating habits may be problematic, and they may explicitly put them on diets. The children need not be seen immediately during an assessment, but they should definitely be involved in the treatment in an age-appropriate fashion.

Terry had experienced tremendous pressure from her mother, who suffered from an eating disorder as well, to maintain a thin shape. After she entered treatment, she became aware of how closely she had been monitoring her own daughter's eating: when she stopped doing so, her daughter promptly gained 10 pounds, but did not continue to gain beyond this.

Families of Origin

While information about the individual families of origin is included in the assessment phase, the inclusion of the patient's family in the therapy may be necessary, particularly if the family is involved in an unhelpful fashion, such as in the example of the mother who continued to take meals to her daughter after her daughter's marriage. In this situation, treating the couple alone would not have been as effective as incorporating family-of-origin sessions separate from the couple sessions. Information needed to make a decision about this must be obtained in the initial assessment. Many married couples cannot readily identify ongoing difficulties with their families of origin, as they had thought that the marriage would somehow eliminate the problems (Roberto, 1991; Root et al., 1986; Schwartz et al., 1985).

Homosexual Couples

Homosexual couples bring into treatment issues and concerns similar to those of heterosexual couples as described earlier, but they also have additional problems. These may include issues such as a recent disclosure of their homosexuality and relationship to their families, and uncertainty about roles due to the acknowledgment of the disorder. In addition, some gay male partners have difficulty understanding the "why," as eating problems are usually thought to be a "woman's disease." Thus, gay and lesbian couples require that interventions be done similar to those done with heterosexual couples.

Ian was involved in a relationship with another man. He was much smaller than his partner, which was preferred by both. Over the first year of their relationship, Ian binged his way to a much higher weight, which was viewed with great alarm by both partners. When Ian presented for treatment, he told his parents about his disorder and his relationship. In addition to concerns about appearance, weight, and shape, the couple had to face the reactions of their families of origin, who had both recently been told of the homosexuality. As it became evident that Ian would want his partner to attend family meetings, he and his partner had to deal with the disclosure of two secrets. Both the patient and partner experienced difficulty dealing with a disorder that is still considered to be primarily a "woman's disease."

Thus, additional education on the disorder is often required during the assessment phase.

Contraindications to Treatment Beyond the Assessment

At the conclusion of the assessment, the therapist will need to determine whether or not couple therapy is indicated, and should review this issue with the couple.

If there is ongoing sexual or physical abuse, it will probably be necessary for the therapist to focus on keeping both members of the couple physically safe, which may delay (or make unnecessary) marital treatment. The severity of the patient's symptoms may be a temporary contraindication to further marital treatment. Patients who are very starved (see Chapter 1) may be unable to concentrate on a marital therapeutic process. If the patient's health is at imminent risk, either because of severe emaciation or from the complications of purging, these concerns may need to be dealt with as a first priority.

A final caution is the presence of a concurrent psychiatric illness, such as depression. Although marital therapy may continue, the patient may need to be referred to a psychiatrist for additional treatment.

SUMMARY

This chapter has focused on the assessment of a couple coming for treatment. Areas that require specific exploration include the couple's understanding of the referral, the illness itself, family-of-origin issues, individual histories, the importance of weight and appearance in the relationship, children, and comorbidity.

A thorough initial assessment in itself can be a significant intervention for a couple, helping them to define areas of concern and to sharpen the focus of their attention. For some couples, the assessment is the first opportunity that the patient and a couple have had to examine the eating problem and its treatment from a more objective perspective. The therapist can help the couple begin to examine ways they can help each other that do not put the patient in a sick and helpless role, with the spouse as the helper. The decision for continued marital therapy should be made jointly by the therapist and the couple. The contraindications to such a recommendation were discussed.

5

Brief Couple Treatment for Eating Disorders

This chapter examines brief marital therapy with couples who are either married or living together, and in which at least one spouse has an eating-disorder diagnosis. The model presented has been used in an institutional setting within the context of the Eating Disorders Day Hospital Program (Piran & Kaplan, 1990), a time-limited, intensive, focused group-therapy program. Different groups in the program focus on specific issues, including body image, nutrition (Kerr & Piran, 1990), and family relations (Shekter-Wolfson & Woodside, 1990). In addition to group therapy, patients are offered family-of-origin therapy, and when the patient is married, marital therapy (Woodside & Shekter-Wolfson, 1991). Although this model was developed for use in the Day Hospital Program, it is equally applicable to a general outpatient clinic or private practice. However, it is also important that the patient be followed medically, which includes monitoring the patient's nutritional status.

The brief marital therapy model is goal-directed and relatively short in duration, that is, between 8 and 10 sessions. Extrasessional tasks are assigned to assist and solidify the change process. In an outpatient practice, these sessions could be spread over six- to seven-month periods, allowing more time for the homework tasks. The focus of treatment is an improvement in the quality of the marital relationship, rather than therapy for the identified patient with a passive, nonparticipatory partner (Andersen, 1985). As with Haley, there is an assumption in this chapter that the individual's problem, in this case the eating disorder, is part of a sequence of acts among several people. "It is the repeating sequence of behavior that is the focus of therapy" (Haley, 1976, p. 2). For example, when the spouse reports that he is monitoring every morsel that the patient eats, or is preparing all of the meals with the hope of getting the patient to eat, the therapist should assist both the patient and spouse to change their behavioral sequence and to organize themselves differently at mealtime. As soon as eating issues are addressed, couple issues—such as problem solving, communication, child care, and sexuality—can be dealt with. Usually this happens at or near the conclusion of this therapy. It is important to keep in mind that the model presented in this chapter can be viewed by itself, or it may be considered as part of a sequence in which longer-term therapy (Chapter 6) will play a role.

BRIEF MARITAL TREATMENT

Overview

Presenting couples in which one spouse has an eating disorder mayleave the therapist feeling that they don't know where to begin. As the eating disorder can be life-threatening, the early focus on the patient's eating, weight, and general health is inevitable and unavoidable (see Chapter 4). However, in addition to the pragmatic aspects of food and eating, the symptoms must also be viewed as a metaphor for the couple's relationship—how they communicate and how they deal with issues of control. Furthermore, the patient's own family may very well be involved in the feeding process.

As well, the therapist may want to look at the issues of couple security, intimacy, guilt, and blame, particularly if the patient had been abused as a child and the trustworthiness of her spouse is a problem.

In the brief therapy model, the timing of when to intervene becomes as important as the range of problems presented. The issues worked with can usually be grouped into three main areas: inclusion and boundaries, control, and intimacy (Table 5.1). Doherty and his colleagues (1984, 1985) advocated that these issues can be organized into a logical hierarchy called the Fundamental Interpersonal Relations Orientation model, or FIRO. The category of inclusion centers around membership in the family treatment process and boundaries. Control issues include responsibility, discipline, power, decision making, and role negotiation. Intimacy issues include open self-disclosure, friendship, and trust. "The model suggests that . . . intimacy issues are generally unresolvable in the presence of strong control struggles . . . and control struggles are difficult to resolve (Doherty & Harkaway, 1990, p. 289).

The goal of brief marital therapy, using the stages outlined, is to help the couple evolve to the point where eating and weight are no longer the main focus and where the couple can begin to address other issues regarding their relationship. Therefore, inclusion and control issues are emphasized more than intimacy issues. At the conclusion of brief marital therapy, the patient and spouse may not be symptom-free, but ideally, improvement in the individual's treatment program will be paralleled by progress in the marital relationship (Andersen, 1985, p. 144).

TABLE 5.1.
Stages of Brief Marital Treatment

1. Defining inclusion and boundaries
2. Negotiating control
3. Achieving intimacy

Inclusion and Boundaries

Issues related to inclusion predominate in the first stage of brief marital therapy. The structural model of Minuchin (1974), which highlights the use of boundary and boundary terminology to define membership in subgroups of larger systems, is most helpful here.

According to this model, couples delineate boundaries through "repeated transactions which establish how, when and to whom to relate" (Minuchin, 1974, p. 51). These transactions, which define who the patient is in relation to her spouse and family of origin, and who the spouse is in relation to the patient, are those that the therapist can study in order to help the couple with their sense of who is included in their family life.

In commenting on families with obese members, Doherty and Harkaway (1990) note that the primary issues of inclusion are "matters of loyalty, alliances, in maintaining membership in the family, and interpersonal bonding." In these families, "obesity comes to mean sameness; thinness signals difference" (p. 291). In families in which a member has BN, the eating disorder often plays a role in the inclusion/exclusion process. For the bulimic patient, being thin may signal her desire for independence and differentiation, while at the same time she is terrified of giving full expression to it and risk being excluded by her family. Unfortunately, the effort to maintain this pseudoindependence via dieting and its sequelae, such as bingeing and purging, leads not only to serious physical problems but also to reactions on the part of the family of origin and spouse that increase their tendency to become too concerned over and too close to the patient.

In the case of the anorexic, thinness is very often valued by most of the members of the family, and the patient's symptoms are ego-syntonic to the system (Schwartz et al., 1985; Root et al., 1986). Externally, the patient may be viewed by her family members as sharing their beliefs, although internally this may not be the case. In these scenarios, as long as the patient behaves in a way that is appropriate to the family norms, familial differences may be minimized. Selvini-Palazzoli described an anorexic family whose motto was, "All for one, and one for all" (Selvini-Palazzoli, et al., 1978). Unfortunately, as the illness becomes more severe and is finally acknowledged, the level of involvement of other members will shift to a consistent monitoring status. For some patients, this overinvolvement can be comforting; others may view it as an intrusion. If the marital relationship was established after the onset of the eating disorder, patterns in the marital relationship are likely to mimic those established in the family of origin.

In families historically struggling with issues of boundary or inclusion, matters are brought to a head when a daughter marries or moves in with a partner. Also, the unresolved inclusion and boundary issues in the family of origin are likely to be replicated in the new relationship. For some, marriage may be viewed as a subtle betrayal of the family. Therefore, being thin or sick may serve to keep the family of origin involved while the patient attains a semblance of independence. It is not surprising that an eating disorder often begins when the individual is making the decision to leave home (Root et al., 1986, p. 103).

> Alice (introduced in Chapters 3 and 4) was a young woman who developed AN around the time she became engaged to be married, her weight reaching its lowest point on her wedding day. The family's and husband's focus was on one specific symptom, her profound abdominal pain; they voiced ambivalent feelings about her diagnosis of AN and hesitated about her admission to an eating-disorders program. The patient had an extremely close relationship with her mother. The couple was offered the opportunity to live in the same community as the patient's parents, but in the house of her husband's recently deceased grandmother. The husband's decision to accept this offer enraged Alice, who had hoped to live closer to her mother. Shortly after the marriage, Alice began to spend increasing amounts of time at her mother's house, which created further friction between Alice and her husband. It was later revealed that she was ashamed of her physical symptoms and did not want anyone to know about them, particularly her in-laws.

Roberto (1986) conceptualizes the patient's dilemma regarding loyalties and inclusion in terms of family legacy. She defines the legacy as "that which is handed down, like a gift, from one's ancestors" (p. 232). She states further that "in families with bulimia, the multi-generational legacy often revolved around weight, attractiveness, fitness and success, and eating of food" (p. 237). Roberto suggests that the therapist can use the family's metaphors and language to reconstruct this legacy, which in turn reflects the family's own values and its definitions of inclusion and boundary. This is useful not only in the first phase of treatment, but in the control and intimacy stages of therapy as well.

The Bates family contained a strong legacy of role definitions. Traditionally, the men and women "separated" when the women became ill. The men freed themselves by becoming involved in work and male leisure activities. Ursula developed AN in her late teens and married Jack at the age of 20. Jack initially was very supportive, taking time off from work and policing Ursula at home. However, by the end of the first year he was beginning to talk of having his own life, and at the time Ursula presented for treatment, the couple was essentially leading separate lives.

One of the first tasks for the marital therapist as far as inclusion is concerned is to decide who should be involved in which aspect of treatment. For couples such as Ursula and Jack, the patient's family of origin might need to be seen in conjunction with the couple's treatment.

Another boundary issue to be dealt with early in treatment is who is responsible for the patient's weight and eating. The patient's weight, health status, and eating pattern should be considered her responsibility, independent of her siblings, parents, and husband. Although this approach may produce a negative response from the spouse or family, it is ultimately crucial, even in the case of very ill patients who either have reached a very low weight or are exhibiting dangerous purging behaviors.

Veronica, a young woman with a 15-year history of AN and BN, employed ipecac as a purgative; she had consumed many hundreds of doses, and had some evidence of the lethal cardiomyopathy that accompanies ipecac use. Her fiancé, himself a bulimic, could not accept that he should halt his frequent searches of her medicine cabinet and drawers in attempts to prevent her further use of ipecac.

The temptation to recruit spouses into the monitoring process may be very great in situations in which the patient's condition is life-threatening or where he or she appears particularly out of control. However, in our experience, this temptation should always be resisted.

The therapist should explore the importance of weight, and shape within the couple's or family's context to see whether these variables are important for belonging to or being included in the family. For example, the therapist may ask what it has been like for the spouse since his wife gained some weight. Any change in eating or other behavior related to weight or shape, such as atemporary halt to exercising or the patient's preparation of meals, should be explored as well. The couple may feel that they may have less in common as the patient begins to shift her usual activity away from an exclusive and previously shared focus on eating, weight, and shape. In addition, being thin or sick may have delayed major life decisions, such as to have children, to move away from the family, or to develop a separate social network. All of these issues may become contentious matters once the patient's eating begins to improve.

The following example illustrates how one therapist included both the family of origin and the spouse around the issue of food.

Wanda, the patient, suffered from BN that she had developed in middle age. She had a daughter who also had BN and two older sisters who were heavy. She came to treatment only after her daughter had acknowledged her own bulimia, and was success-fully treated. Wanda, a dancer, ate in a restrictive fashion in her early married life. However, she did not appear to develop a formal eating disorder until later. She and her husband, Karl, frequently ate at the home of Wanda's parents, where Wanda's mother monitored her eating to ensure that she was eating enough so that she would not be so thin. After Wanda became pregnant, she continued to be "fed" by her mother, who was quite overweight herself. Following the birth of her second child, Wanda became bulimic and gained weight. She was unable to vomit and used diuretics to regulate her weight. Her mother was pleased with her daughter's weight gain, but still continued to bring her food. Wanda felt frustrated because she was unable to "purge" her mother's food adequately.

After assessing the couple, it seemed important to include Wanda's mother in the therapy process, as issues around eating could not be resolved without her mother's presence. Wanda's father had died two years earlier, prior to the therapeutic encounter. In an interview with the couple and Wanda's mother, the mother talked about her daughter's weight problem and how she helped her daughter gain weight. She felt that her daughter's weight at the time of her marriage was far too low. Wanda's mother seemed to be outlining a family legacy about weight maintenance that was important to pass on to her child. The therapist felt that challenging the mother's feeding (control) without addressing the importance of inclusion and belonging would have been premature. The therapist then explored the importance of Wanda's weight and eating for the family of origin. There seemed to be a connection between her feeding and being needed, between eating and accepting care. It was also noted that Wanda's mother spent very little time with her other two daughters; it seemed as though they did not need her any longer.

Wanda's mother was encouraged to look at other ways in which all her daughters could benefit from a mother and grandmother (since her daughters all had children). In other words, the therapist was addressing the issue of inclusion and belonging and suggesting a different form of relational boundary appropriate for this phase of the family life cycle. In addition, the therapist attempted to redirect Wanda's sense of "loyalty" away from eating and shape and toward other ways in which the mother and daughter could feel close.

Karl was encouraged to become involved in some of the activities planned for Wanda and her mother, so as to deemphasize the mother–daughter link and reestablish the mother/mother-in-law and couple link.

There are times when inclusion issues appear more important to the therapist than to the couple. This occurs when families of origin are geographically distant or totally uninvolved and cut off. Couples who have little to do with their families may feel that an autonomous status has been achieved simply by virtue of their minimal contact or physical distance. To such a couple, even the suggestion to include the family of origin would seem senseless, in that they do not see themselves as being influenced in any way by their families. "We have not seen our families in years," is a common response to the question of independence and autonomy.

Unfortunately, these attitudes are seen when the couple or patient is fearful and very reactive to the family's feelings and opinions, and can only achieve a sense of separateness when totally cut off. This pattern, which is typical of avoidant, insecure families, may repeat itself in the marital relationship, and will have an adverse effect on intimacy. Interestingly, confusion between a sense of autonomy and of being cut off from one's family of origin is not all that dissimilar to the anorexic's or bulimic's dichotomous view of herself vis-à-vis food. She may pride herself on being in control, but in reality is totally enslaved by her fear of food.

Susan (described in Chapter 4) had very little contact with her family of origin; yet she was very close to her fiancé's large family. She had been triangulated and parentified into her parents' chronic and very severe marital difficulties, and decided that she herself was a significant perpetuator of these difficulties. At the time of her admission to the Day Hospital Program, she had been engaged for several months, but had not informed her parents that she planned to marry.

In working with the couple described here, the therapist felt that the patient's family of origin had to be acknowledged. Through the patient's exploration of her family relationships, she identified a sense of exclusion from family membership.

The patient was encouraged to include her parents in a session. They knew nothing of her pending marriage, and they had never met her fiancé. Initially the patient was reluctant to include her parents or to divulge the upcoming marriage, but she was encouraged by her boyfriend. The major focus of this session was to help the patient and family connect. One of the patient's fears was that her mother would become overinvolved once she was told that her daughter was sick; in a sense, going from one extreme to the other. The therapist's role was to help clarify boundaries between the mother and the daughter. One of these tasks included having the daughter simply "tell" her mother about her wedding plans, as a method of beginning to establish limits in the mother–daughter relationship. The patient felt that it was too premature to "ask" her mother for assistance in planning the wedding. It was going to take time to complete the process of delineating the nature of the relationship.

Control

The second stage of brief marital therapy involves addressing control issues, such as the spouse's relationship with the patient's illness and the negotiation of family-of-origin issues. The therapist has gathered information from the assessment stage about both the spouse's and the family of origin's role in the preparation of food and overall "feeding" of the patient (see Chapter 4). Struggles around food in the marriage can be viewed in the content of a battle for control not only between the patient and her food, but also between the patient and her spouse. These struggles may be a recent addition to the marriage, or they may have been present since the inception of the relationship. Haley (1976) states: "When an individual shows symptoms, the organization has a hierarchical arrangement that is confused. It may be confused by being ambiguous, so that no one knows who is the peer and who is his superior" (p. 103). In other words, who or what (e.g., chaotic eating) is really in control often shifts or is obscure. Haley's strategic model helps the therapist to work with a couple where "resistance" and struggles are the norm. "To motivate someone to do something means to persuade the person that there is some gain for him" (Haley, 1976, p. 54). One way to reduce resistance is to introduce small steps so that the couple will feel successful, rather than moving directly to an ideal held by the therapist.

Symptom Separation

Thus, in the second stage, the therapist tries to help the spouse and patient relieve the struggles around food or eating, recognizing that it will take time. This may be a difficult stage of the treatment, as the patient's ability to take responsibility for her own eating may be far from solidified at this point. This stage is referred to as symptom separation (Schwartz et al., 1985). Schwartz and colleagues suggest that "the degree to which the spouse is able to disengage from the symptom is often a prognostic indication of the rigidity and enmeshment of the couple" (p. 295). The therapist should anticipate resistance, and even hostility, particularly if the spouse has been intimately involved with the problem for a long time. Illnesses present at the time of marriage may stabilize a relationship that otherwise would not have survived by acting as psychological "glue" for the ill member or for the spouse (Andersen, 1985). In this situation, a symptom separation may create tremendous imbalance and be viewed as threatening the marriage. If the illness occurs after the establishment of the relationship or the marriage, it is likely that the spouse will not be invested in the symptoms, and will find them more frustrating and puzzling. In these situations, its onset is often seen at the time of a marital crisis, such as moving, the birth of an unwanted child, difficulties around controlling the children, or an extramarital affair (see Chapter 4).

Symptom separation focuses on fostering the patient's nascent sense of assertiveness and autonomy. The spouse, patient, and family of origin find themselves caught up in a vicious circle. The spouse's many attempts to "feed" the patient may not have allowed the patient to "feed herself." In this context, "feeding" can be best viewed as a metaphor for difficulties in providing interpersonal nurturance and support within the couple's relationship. Lacking other tools to provide a sense of supportiveness, those faced with ill and struggling spouses may feel they have no other choice than to intervene directly in the patient's eating behaviors. The "overly rich emotional connectedness between a bulimic individual and her partner creates an interdependency like the meshing of gears" (Roberto, 1991, p. 74). Thus, when the identified patient makes attempts toward greater self-expression, the "connected" parties inevitably experience this shift as a break in the connection, and all parties may become more distressed as a result of the insecurity. (This process occurred with Alice, described above.) Therefore, it is important to assist the spouse in tolerating a "symptom separation" by carefully framing the intervention as one likely to be helpful to the couple, rather than as a simple instruction to back off from the patient.

Symptom separation moves the couple to clarify their boundaries, and also serves as a potent intervention in the realm of control. Although symptom separation challenges the spouse to redefine his relationship vis-à-vis the patient by removing himself from one aspect of the patient's struggle, it does not give the spouse permission to become uncaring or uninvolved. Rather, it is designed to help the spouse and patient relate to each other without one partner's being defined as sick and the other as in control.

Yvonne, bulimic for several decades, was separated from Larry. Both denied that the eating disorder was connected to the separation in any way. Larry continued to see Yvonne socially, usually taking her out to dinner. She would excuse herself at the end of each meal, and invariably vomit. While suspicious, Larry never confronted Yvonne or stopped taking her out to dinner.

A very basic type of symptom separation involves labeling. The therapist indicates behaviors that will be helpful for the couple and those unlikely to be helpful. Unproductive behaviors include advising each other to diet, locking refrigerators, and hiding food. Labeling may seem to be a simplistic intervention, but the couple often experiences it as sensible and helpful. Suggestions should be phrased in language the couple understands.

Zoe had been living with her boyfriend, Manny, for one year. Food and control were very relevant issues in both the family of origin and her present living situation, as Zoe's family owned and ran a restaurant, and her boyfriend had been a cook. Most of Zoe's bingeing and purging occurred in the family restaurant. Zoe was working at the restaurant full-time and going to school part-time to learn accounting. Manny did not like Zoe's being out of the house so much, and he felt that he would be better able to help her if she stayed home more.

In working with this couple, several control issues were addressed. First, there were difficulties in determining which of the partners was in charge. As a result, their relationship was very reactive. Zoe felt that Manny was trying to manipulate her by monitoring all her moves and her time away from home. When he found out about her bulimia, he insisted that he cook for her. Until that point, she had eaten with him only on rare occasions. The second issue involved Zoe's family of origin. The family was faced with a sudden "symptom separation" when Zoe agreed to come into the Day Hospital Program, which prevented her from working at the restaurant during the week. The therapist felt that it would be advantageous to work with both systems (the family of origin and the couple). It would not have been appropriate to suggest that

Zoe totally withdraw from the restaurant, as membership and boundary issues were very relevant in this family business. Yet her bingeing and purging took place there. On the other hand, Manny was prepared to remain at home and cook for her on the weekends, the only feasible time for her to work in the family restaurant.

In this case, the therapist met with Zoe and her parents without Manny, and then met with Zoe and Manny together with the family of origin. The therapist focused on understanding Zoe's father's role in the business, which had been handed down to him by his own father. The therapist learned that one of Zoe's brothers had not wanted anything to do with the business, and, in turn, the father had little to do with him.

The father agreed that Zoe was very good at bookkeeping. With this in mind, it was suggested that Zoe work on the restaurant books. Her schooling would provide valuable skills for the business. Bookkeeping would keep her connected to the restaurant and not leave her feeling as though she were being controlled. In addition, the father could see this as mutually beneficial. Thus the father would continue to run the family business and she would be a financial consultant. Zoe's decision regarding her ultimate future in the restaurant did not have to be made at that time.

Manny had more difficulty around issues of control. His resistant style and his unemployed status aggravated an already difficult situation. In this case, the couple alternated between wanting to break up and wanting to stay together. The therapist addressed Manny's feeling of helplessness and low self-esteem as a way of connecting with him. Manny prided himself on being an excellent cook, and yet his girlfriend did not want to eat his food. It was agreed that the couple would decide on an evening when he would prepare dinner for just the two of them. The meal would be reframed as their special time, rather than as Manny's taking care of her. For her part, Zoe was to help create the mood with candles, music, and so on.

Meal Sessions as an Intervention

When control issues are being dealt with in the marital therapy, a meal session with the couple or with the couple and family of origin together may be useful. If the couple has children, a family meal provides a good opportunity to experience the issues that are operating. The meal session can allow the therapist to experience the couple's struggles around eating, and to intervene with some problem-solving techniques.

The timing of the meal session is important. As was mentioned in Chapter 4, our format for meal sessions is a variant of that described by Minuchin et al. (1978). It is essential that the meal session not place either the spouse or the patient in a position of helplessness. Before setting up the session, the therapist should ask about the timing of meals at home, the participants, and the current eating rituals.

Because Wanda's mother was very involved with her eating, the therapist chose to include her mother in the couple's meal session. The mother was asked to cook the meal for the session because she usually cooked for the couple. The presession directive for Wanda was to avoid any form of purging. The mother, who readily agreed to the meal session, quickly included the therapist as a family member. As her mother served the meal, Wanda said that she would rather serve herself, a departure from the usual routine. The mother was initially shocked, but continued to attempt to serve Wanda. Wanda's husband, Karl, appeared to be very uncomfortable at this point, and made some attempt to rescue his wife; the therapist suggested that he allow his wife to resolve this issue on her own. Wanda again responded to her mother with a "No" as she again attempted to serve her. At this point, the mother turned to the therapist and asked what she should do next. The therapist encouraged the mother to redirect her comment to her daughter.

Later in the session, the therapist reframed the daughter's "No" from being the retort of a bad daughter, to Wanda's way of saying,

"I need to learn this now if I am to pass the expertise on to my children." The mother's expertise as a cook, feeder, and nurturer was acknowledged. The therapist suggested that her knowledge of cooking had to be passed down so that the next generation could learn. This reframing allowed the family to feel validated and secure. The control issue with the mother could shift from one-up/one-down to a more reciprocal relationship, providing a model for the marriage.

Intimacy

Matters of intimacy, such as sexuality, self-disclosure, and mutual sharing, become available for discussion late in the course of brief work with the couple. In many instances, this material will only be touched upon lightly and highlighted for the couple, to be taken up later if they so wish. While this may seem artificial in the light of our need in the Day Hospital Program to discharge patients after a certain length of time, many therapists will work in settings where brief treatments are the norm, for either financial or personnel reasons. It should be recognized that work on the area of intimacy can take a long time. Although couples may be referred for further treatment at the termination of brief therapy, they may not follow through immediately. Some couples will be "stuck" in dealing with boundary or control issues. Some will have experienced increased marital distress as eating has begun to improve, and fear further deterioration in their relationship as a consequence of additional treatment. In other situations, the increased level of intimacy the couple experiences during the identified patient's beginning recovery may be frightening to the couple. Finally, some couples may simply have "had enough" treatment and wish a break from the in-depth examination of their relationship.

However, some couples are prepared for further treatment. The issues they may wish to explore include sexuality, abuse, and family-of-origin relationships. For example, the weight gain of the patient with AN may have an impact on her feeling attractive. She may question why her husband would want to make love to someone who looks like her. Ironically, the couple's previous sexual relationship may have been limited or nonexistent, as the patient is likely to have felt unattractive while ill. If the patient was abused as a child, this may become an active issue for the couple. The couple may also wish to explore other family-of-origin issues. The discussion around control or inclusion may have begun a process that both the patient and spouse may want to continue.

With the introduction of the intimacy phase, the couple is clearly moving into a new contractual relationship with the therapist. It is often the case that formal recontracting will occur at this time.

SUMMARY

This chapter described a model of brief couple treatment for patients with eating disorders that focuses primarily on work with issues of boundary and inclusion and of interpersonal control. Although this form of intervention is relatively new and unexplored, it seems to assist the patient, her spouse, and her family to work toward overcoming the illness and diminishing the feelings of hopelessness it involves. It is the patient's relationship that is placed at center stage in this intervention, not the eating disorder. The eating symptoms are utilized to bring the relationship into sharper focus. The goals of brief marital therapy are to help the patient and her spouse feel responsible for their own areas of difficulty and to be supportive of each other.

6

Long-Term Treatment of Eating-Disordered Couples

This chapter is based on our clinical experience with the long-term treatment and supervision of treatment of couples with an eating-disordered member.

The literature on the long-term treatment of couples with eating disorders is limited, and case reports of long-term individual treatment of an eating-disordered member of a couple occasionally refer to marital difficulties, but do not deal with the marital system specifically (Andersen, 1985).

Many couples with an eating-disordered member initiate longer-term treatment after an initial contact for brief treatment of either the eating disorder or their marital difficulties. Usually, either the short-term treatment was unable to ameliorate the eating disorder, or it effected some change in the eating-disordered member that led to the destabilization of the marriage. Other couples seek long-term treatment as the result of a referral for marital difficulties in which the eating disorder was not seen to be significant by the couple or their referral source. Whether or not there has been an initial phase of treatment, the therapist must reassess the couple and the illness in order to plan a course of action.

ASSESSMENT

Therapeutic Stance

Before outlining the assessment of the couple, we will describe the therapist's stance, which plays an important role in maximizing the therapist's helpfulness to the couple throughout the course of therapy. This therapeutic stance is based on a systemic understanding of the nature of the loyalty dynamics, the insecure attachment pattern, the relational imbalances, and the shame-bound nature of the eating-disordered family.

The therapist is best served by assuming a welcoming position with relation to the couple, indicating that the early meetings are designed to determine whether the therapist has the means to be of help to the couple. This approach allows the couple to experience themselves as part of a treatment system that is not so much judging as collaborating with them to decide whether marital work can help them in dealing with their problems. The therapist and the couple must feel comfortable with the conclusion that help can or cannot be provided by the therapist and that other approaches may also be useful.

A systemic, multimodal approach is best suited to working with the eating-disordered couple because, in most cases, a collection of therapeutic techniques will be required at various stages in the treatment. These techniques, mentioned later in the chapter, might include individual therapy, group therapy, medications, and hospitalization.

Often the therapist is called upon to state a position on the validity or viability of the marriage. As one husband of an anorextic/bulimic wife asked, "You can be honest with me, do you think this marriage has a chance?" A variation of this question is to ask the therapist to take responsibility for the marriage. A husband of an anorexic wife said, "Doc, this marriage is two minutes to midnight . . . what are you going to do about it?" It is best for the therapist to reassure the couple that the work to be undertaken is neither for nor against the marriage and that the decisions about the marriage belong to them alone. They can be informed that therapy should help them develop, grow, and confront the troubling problems they face, but that the therapist will not participate in the decision-making process when it comes to the marital relationship.

The therapeutic stance must be frank, open, and partial to the positions of both members of the couple. This can be difficult if the eating-disordered member is extremely symptomatic early in treatment and is unable or unwilling to participate fully because of such problems as emaciation, medical difficulties, or severe depression. Any medical or psychiatric emergencies must be addressed first, before the relational dynamics of the couple can be dealt with directly. The therapist's attention to such matters as medical problems can serve to help the couple restore some of its relational balance and allow the parentified spouse, who often is involved in helping the eating-disordered partner, to relinquish his anxiety and control in the relationship. A nonmedical therapist should have a close liaison with an attuned medical colleague who can deal with these matters. A stance of multilateral partiality (Boszormenyi-Nagy & Krasner, 1986) allows both members of the couple to be securely connected with the therapist and the therapist to be in a position to side with all members of the family. This allows the development of a secure and respectful environment in which each individual's problems can be aired, explored, and resolved. As the basis of the work with the couple requires that problems be owned and confronted, the security of the therapeutic relationship is paramount.

Issues in the Assessment Process

Some therapists prefer to see members of the couple individually as well as together during the assessment period. Although this may seem useful when the eating-disordered individual appears embarrassed to reveal details of her disorder to the spouse and when the spouse is hesitant to reveal his own maladaptive behavior in the presence of an overtly ill partner, we find that the conjoint session offers the greatest potential for building security and trust. Individual work is best done after a marital treatment contract has evolved, unless the conjoint work leads to the finalization of a decision to separate or proves too disruptive because of mutual blaming and hostility.

Early in the assessment process, it is vital to help the couple begin to identify feelings, including shame, embarrassment, anger, fear, and sadness, and to contextualize them as tools to promote self-understanding and growth. A high prevalence of severe personality disorders in both members of these couples necessitates such identification and contextualization. Otherwise, affective responses elicited in the course of normal history taking will serve to alienate, disorient, and frighten rather than to encourage therapeutic work. Shame, for instance, is often mislabeled as anxiety, anger, confusion, boredom, or tension. When unrecognized feelings, particularly shame, arise in a therapy session and are not responded to, the level of security in the therapeutic relationship diminishes, which impedes communication. As indicated in earlier chapters, shame and its many faces are central to the eating-disordered system, and, as noted by other workers, must be constantly and quickly addressed (Fossum & Mason, 1986).

> Amanda, a 28-year-old married woman with BN, came to the second session with her husband, looking disheveled and agitated. Her husband furiously accused her of staying out late the previous night and cruising the local bars. Amanda did not speak until she was asked why she chose to spend the night out. At first, she asked for her husband to leave the room, but then decided that it would be possible to talk about herself in his presence. She said that she had to cruise because she was feeling so bad about herself and because she couldn't face coming to a session and talking about her bingeing and purging behavior.

Two other matters are also important, as they establish, early on, the safety and respectfulness of the working environment: secrets and accessibility to the therapist. Secret discussions with the therapist and the harboring of secrets are not useful for treatment. Often the secret is a means of avoiding shame or preventing the dissolution of the relationship. Trust and security are enhanced when secrets are shared in a respectful, partial space. Secretiveness is central to the eating disorder itself, particularly around such matters as dieting, food fads, bingeing, and weight-loss techniques (Herzog, 1982). Andersen's description of the bulimic individual alludes to this and to the consequent guilt and shame:

> The essential feature of patients who qualify for the diagnosis of bulimia is that they experience their binges as alien, foreign, and repugnant, but feel unable to gain any effective control over them. Their lives are marked by shame and guilt and by complicated, secretive patterns devised to allow them to continue their practice without public notice. The secretiveness is not like that of a person sneaking away to have a pleasant, recreational drug experience, but more like that of a driven person who feels impelled to perform something against his or her will. (Andersen, 1985, p. 114)

It is important that the therapist indicate to the couple that the presence of secrets about eating is to be expected, and that these secrets, rather than shielding the partner, actually interfere with the partners' ability to develop trust in each other.

Occasionally, there are secrets other than those involving food and eating that are difficult for couples to handle. As the marital relationship is usually based on an implicit or explicit agreement about sexual fidelity, the presence of a secret affair is a serious matter. Even if the couple is aware of infidelity, open discussion is extremely threatening because it leaves the couple vulnerable to feelings of enormous shame (Pittman, 1989). If the couple has provided the therapist with a history of sexual difficulty, it is useful for the therapist to broach the topic by asking: "In view of the serious problems you had in trying to develop your sexual relationship, has either of you turned to other sexual partners?" Although this question can produce a good deal of discomfort, it nonetheless signals to the couple that safe discussion about this topic is sanctioned in the therapeutic setting.

Accessibility to the therapist is another critical issue to address early in the assessment phase. By providing the couple with clear directions for access and a reliable access schedule, the therapist can avoid the anxious security checks often iatrogenically induced when he or she adopts a distant, inaccessible position. Clear and reliable scheduling of sessions, with reliable beginnings and endings, and the provision of a phone number where the therapist can be reached are often sufficient. Telling patients to call if, in their judgment, they have a problem that is proving too difficult to deal with is often quite useful.

During the assessment, it is important to obtain a good family and developmental history of both members of the couple. In addition to allowing each member of the couple to tell his or her story in a supported, respectful environment, it allows the listening partner to learn more about his or her spouse. The data gathered are invaluable both in understanding the roots of the insecurity, relational imbalance, and shame in the couple and in allowing each individual to begin to recognize the importance and uniqueness of his or her own story.

Finally, it is crucial to identify as many of the couple's compulsive/addictive behaviors as soon as possible. This is important because the eating disorder is often just one of the behaviors related to the basic sense of insecurity in the couple that have the potential of derailing the therapeutic process.

Amanda (described above) was a 28-year-old mother of three. She had severe BN, and also was a compulsive clothes shopper, sun tanner (four times a week), and drinker. Her husband used both hashish and alcohol compulsively. Their drinking episodes and Amanda's shopping episodes were used to avoid facing the serious doubts that both had about the marriage and their suitability for one another. Each partner's family of origin disapproved of the marriage.

With the Cohens, on the other hand, the husband was a compulsive worker and exerciser, and the wife, as part of her anorexic picture, was a compulsive exerciser. Their rigorous schedules allowed them to avoid any confrontation and any form of intimacy.

These data are of great importance as the eating-disordered individual, and often her spouse, uses these compulsive behaviors secretly as a way to assuage inexpressible or unmentionable feelings, which she and her spouse have enormous difficulties in labeling and contextualizing in their lives and in the relationship.

The inability to perceive inner feeling states (hunger, anxiety, sadness, or anger) and the greater ability to exercise will to control urges to eat characterize the food restricting anorectic patient. In contrast, greater awareness of inner states and/or lessened ability to control urges and impulses characterizes the bulimic personality, independent of other features. (Andersen, 1985, p. 110)

In order to begin the process of helping the anorextic to label and experience her feelings and the bulimic to gain some control over feelings that are often poorly understood and so are overpowering, the therapist has to assist the couple to acknowledge and begin to deal with the compulsive behaviors. This may require the use of ancillary help such as drug or alcohol abuse counseling, often before working on the eating disorder itself.

Ancillary Consultation During Assessment

In addition to developing an understanding of the couple's history and the history of each member's individual problems, it is important to delineate the areas of responsibility for various elements in the couple's care. If there is any evidence of a serious psychiatric disorder in either partner, this must be evaluated by appropriate consultants and treated in conjunction with the therapy. Medical problems that might arise from either the bulimia or anorexia also must be addressed through referral to qualified physicians.

TREATMENT

Once treatment is agreed upon, the eating disorder itself takes center stage. Usually experienced as autonomous in relation to the dynamics that activated it, the disorder also maintains those very dynamics—namely, insecurity, shame, and a sense of lost control. As most eating-disordered individuals have had some short-term therapy prior to beginning long-term work, the eating disorder may be "out of control," and either inpatient or day hospitalization may be needed to help the eating-disordered individual gain some form of control over the eating symptoms. A degree of control is a central goal of therapy since it opens up the possibility of working with the underlying conflicts and dynamic issues. As Andersen (1985) states: "The goal . . . is to break the repetitive cycle of losing control, and thereby decrease the guilt, shame, and demoralization that result" (p. 126).

In many instances, neither the couple nor the eating-disordered individual is prepared for such a great commitment because of its disruption of life and the humiliation of being in a hospital. If the disorder is life threatening or became unmanageable before the seeking of therapy, there is no alternative but to recommend this as a first step to treatment. The therapist must be prepared for this possibility. He or she will have to help the couple understand that the eating disorder has taken on a life of its own, and that, in many cases, it may be too hard for either the eating-disordered individual or the couple to deal with the clinical situation without the use of hospitalization, where the resources of an entire system can be mobilized to address the illness. The therapist, too, must be aware that the eating disorder cannot usually be treated with psychotherapy alone.

Issues in the Early Phase of Therapy

The early phase of treatment often focuses on issues that are also part of brief treatment (see Chapter 5). Decisions about who is to be included in treatment, what constitutes the boundaries of the couple, and the role of the families of origin are usually central. When dealing with insecure, anxious families of origin, the therapist has to be prepared to interact with them in a way that mirrors their concern and shame over the problems that their children, the couple, are facing, while at the same time delineating clear boundaries as to who is involved in the therapy. In some cases, families of origin in which insecure anxious attachment styles predominate will have to be seen more than once to help them alleviate their feelings of insecurity and to build trust in the therapist. Insecure avoidant families will seem not to be very involved until there is a sign of behavioral change in one of the spouses, and they then often become very involved at that point. The case of Alice, described in Chapter 3, provides an example of an avoidant system's becoming overly involved after treatment has had an effect on the couple.

The process of joining commences when the couple is first contacted. This initial phase requires special attention to shame, dietary regulation, and the ongoing patterns of control in the dyad. The eating-disordered patient is placed in charge of her dietary and weight regulation, while the spouse is supported in his withdrawal from this area of concern. This allows two central matters to be addressed: the maladaptive substitution of control for security in the couple's current relationship and the resulting relational imbalances that result when each is forced to give up autonomy in order to comply with and be regulated by the other.

As mentioned earlier, control struggles in the dyad are used by both parties to ensure security and attachment. Thus each partner will require understanding and support in order to give up the controlling behavior and address the often shameful concerns about security. Not only will the spouse have to deal with his attempts to control his wife's eating pattern, but the eating-disordered spouse will also have to address her part in colluding with him. The ownership of problems other than the eating disorder is also a relevant concern early in the work. Thus the husband's drinking, for example, would be framed as a problem that he has to take charge of in the same way that his wife must deal with her eating disorder—by herself.

The establishment of some ownership of symptoms opens the way for the couple to begin to venture outside the relationship to get help with specific matters. Self-help or therapy groups focusing on such problems as body image, self-assertiveness, substance abuse, and sexual abuse can be extremely useful when the noninvolved spouse can adopt a trusting and supportive position toward their use.

In addition to beginning to define the boundaries of the dyad and the goals of their work around the eating disorder, the couple is encouraged to consider ways in which to build their marital relationship. This work allows the therapist to frame the therapeutic enterprise in a positive light. It can be cast as an opportunity to grow and develop personally, rather than as a struggle to cope with their combined inadequacies and badness. The positive frame allows the therapist to help the couple begin to recognize the role of insecurity and shame in their lives and to utilize their strengths in the treatment. It may not be clear until this stage of the work that certain couples will not be amenable to marital therapy. Although the abilities to attend sessions regularly and to maintain basic boundaries are indispensable for undertaking this form of treatment, the couple will have to provide some evidence of wanting to work together and to build their marriage. Where this is not possible, the couple should be referred for group or individual therapy and their decision awaited before marital therapy is attempted.

Material brought to sessions is best dealt with in an experiential manner and connected with historical data that the therapist has collected about the couple. Reference to previous interaction in the session and the construction of metaphors that the couple can share and utilize allow them to signify and share events.

Amanda (to husband): "I can't let you tell me when and what to eat any more!"

Norm: "Well, what about your bingeing . . . OK, OK, you're right. I have to stay out of it."

Therapist: "Good work. This is just like two sessions ago when you [Amanda] decided to stand up for yourself in another way and sat down in the brown chair. And you [Norm] were able to support her then, too."

The following is an example of a metaphor developed by the patient and used in the marital work.

> Bridget, a bulimic woman aged 27, came to treatment with her husband, Owen, age 28. Both were highly verbal and enjoyed verbal play in the sessions. Bridget coined the term "my greedy hunger monster" to explain her prebinge experience. This term was used by her, her husband, and the therapist to discuss, in a playful, non-shaming way, the affective upheaval she experienced many times a week. By describing aspects of this hunger monster, she was able to give voice to parts of herself that she had formerly suppressed.

Accounts of loss and abandonment can be explored for affective intensity by listening carefully to the concrete details about the events that led up to the loss or abandonment. The feelings connected with these events can then be supported and contextualized. Also, the couple's actual interaction in the session can be used to help them reexperience the affects about which they felt shame. The validation and support of affects is crucial, as this helps the members of the couple to develop a sense of trust in themselves and in the therapeutic work, as well as to learn about and empathize with their own feelings.

Couples with children should be seen with the children, either by the marital therapist or by a family therapy consultant early in the work. In addition to allowing the therapist direct observation of family functioning, it provides the children with access to a resource outside the family who is "helping Mom and Dad." This has the effect of reducing the amount of parentification children of all couples who struggle with emotional difficulties experience (Boszormenyi-Nagy & Sparkes, 1973). If there is evidence of severe difficulty in parenting, the therapist must address this issue through referral or by suggesting resources to help with the children. If the parents are managing, the therapist must join them as a coach and resource for problem solving, not as a parent substitute. The couple must remain, as they should in all aspects of the therapeutic work, the executives in control of their lives. The only situations that would merit another approach are those in which the children are in physical or emotional danger (e.g., sexual abuse, physical abuse, or severe neglect).

Issues in the Middle Phase of Treatment

During this phase of treatment, the couple usually begins to elaborate and extend their work on shame, trust, and sexuality. The therapist is less active and serves more as a guide and facilitator for the couple's work. The therapy session is used to provide the couple with a secure base (Byng-Hall, 1990), from which they can explore feelings about themselves, the relationship, and their connection to their families of origin. The family-of-origin work that is most central at this time focuses around the boundaries between the family of origin and the nuclear family, invisible loyalties to the family of origin (Boszormenyi-Nagy & Sparkes, 1973), and the couple's struggle to deal with their families' difficulties with change (Stierlin & Weber, 1989).

The therapist's consistency, reliability, and multilateral partiality are important so that the couple can confront fairness and unfairness in the relationship, particularly where their codependency has enslaved both of them in unwilling caretaker and care-seeker roles, and has perpetuated the relational imbalance that each experienced in the family of origin. The eating-disordered member's concerns about body shape and size, femininity, and sexuality may have to be dealt with in individual therapy before they can be integrated into the couple work. The therapy can be undertaken through a referral, and the couple's work can proceed concurrently.

The therapist must be alert to such problems as drug and alcohol addiction that may be first "discovered" at this juncture in treatment.

These must be addressed as they arise lest they derail treatment. The sequelae of sexual or physical abuse may also become more apparent at this time rather than earlier in the treatment, because of the increased trust and security in the treatment situation. These problems must also be addressed as they are brought up, and when they cannot be dealt with easily in the couple's work, they may require referral for concurrent individual or group therapy.

Issues in the Late Phase of Treatment

As the couple develops a greater sense of intimacy and the eating disorder moves out of its central position in the work, other matters come into focus. First and foremost, there is a concern about termination. This in itself offers a great opportunity to reexamine and rework feelings about loss, shame, and belonging for the couple. The termination of therapy presents both the possibility that access will be denied to an important resource and the opportunity to feel shame when there is recognition that the therapist has come to mean so much to the couple.

As a general observation, although active treatment terminates, the relationship between the therapist and patient remains part of their shared history forever. This fact is a useful one to discuss, and this discussion can alleviate some of the feelings of loss and disconnection to which the couple is so sensitive. Although some forms of treatment advocate a complete cutoff of the client from the therapist, reassurance about access after therapy is over not only is important in preventing the resurgence of symptomatology at this phase of treatment, but is fair to everyone as well.

Concerns about "being dependent" on the therapy or therapist are often shame-based feelings about the awareness that the therapeutic relationship has become important. This can lead to an increasing sense of "stuckness" in the sessions, and ultimately to an early disruption of therapy. The celebration of finding an "important relationship," one that can be a model for many others, is a useful way to alleviate the shame that the awareness invokes. Gifts given to the therapist at this stage of treatment are often expressions of this awareness, as well as tokens of gratitude. They serve to mark or symbolize the experience and, to some extent, to reciprocate for what has been received. The therapist, it is hoped, can accept these gifts gracefully and so validate their importance.

Another important development that may arise early in the treatment and should be supported throughout the therapeutic work is the involvement of the couple, as individuals and as a unit, in communal functioning. Whether these activities involve attending religious services or doing volunteer work for social service or political organizations, they are important for shame-bound family members, who often stay on the fringe of society. They help to normalize the family system and to provide "acceptable pressures" to allow for the movement of the couple into a sphere of life that is separate from those of their families of origin.

Crises

Occasionally, during couple therapy, the couple may decide to dissolve the marriage. The therapist can be helpful by providing the couple with a secure environment in which to discuss this decision, and later as a resource to help with referral to other therapists if the members of the couple wish to continue psychotherapeutic work individually. Continued work with each of the separated partners may be possible, but requires that the estranged partners not feel impeded by or insecure as the result of the therapist's seeing the other partner as well. In addition, the therapist must be prepared to have his or her capacity to be partial taxed to its limit.

As mentioned earlier in the chapter, sexual infidelity is disruptive of the couple treatment and cannot be accepted as a reasonable activity while treatment is ongoing. The basic security that marital (sexual) fidelity provides is a minimal necessity for working with a couple for which issues of attachment and loss are so sensitive. In the event that this becomes an issue during treatment, it is best dealt with in a nonmoralistic manner.

Therapist: "We can't work together while Cecile is having an affair. The process doesn't work under these conditions."

The reason for the infidelity is important to understand, and the behavior itself, when it becomes known, will have to be discussed in the context of the relationship.

The medical sequelae of AN and BN that become evident during therapy sessions must be attended to. It is crucial for a therapist who is not a physician to maintain a liaison with a medical resource (hospital, family practitioner, internist) that can monitor the eating-disordered individual and provide medical care when necessary. A physician-therapist is often in a better position to evaluate the medical nature of the patient's complaints during therapy, but can benefit from the help of a medical colleague in managing and monitoring the medical sequelae of these conditions (see Chapter 1).

Countertransference to the Couple

The very nature of these marital systems leaves the therapist open to three major countertransference responses that can impede therapy: shame, control, and caretaking.

The shame-bound nature of the family and couple systems often induces insecurity and shame in the therapist. When this happens, the therapist also can react in a shame-based way. For example, the therapist's own feelings about any difficulties in the therapeutic work can lead to feelings of shame and to functioning in a secretive manner similar to that in which the family deals with its shortcomings. This results in the ineffective use of consultation, supervision, and ancillary treatment to help the couple with their problems. The therapist can guard against this by working with a group of therapists and sharing discussions of problems with colleagues, while, at the same time, respecting the patient's confidentiality.

When struggles for control are not seen as struggles for security and trust, the therapist may become authoritarian, and, by taking over, generate a great deal of shame and humiliation on the part of the patients in the treatment process. This stance increases the sense of helplessness and lack of self-control that the patient and her spouse feel, and minimizes the effectiveness of the therapy. Only when life-threatening situations arise should the therapist take over. By organizing a "contract" regarding "takeover points" in advance, while the patient is in an executive position, the therapist can prepare for those times where the patient and her spouse are helplessly caught up in the turmoil of her symptomatology. These "takeover points" usually require the patient to go into a hospital for care when she has reached a dangerously low body weight or shows signs of a severely disturbed metabolism. With a contract in place, the therapist can act as an agent for a patient who gave anticipatory consent to this action while in a less symptomatic phase of her illness.

Finally, when codependency is central to the relationship, the therapist may become involved in conflicts around usurping caretaking patterns that have provided at least a modicum of security for the couple. Put simply, the therapist must be aware that he or she can be neither a better wife, husband, father, or mother for either member of the couple than the one who is already in place. In general, all parenting and caregiving must ultimately come from within the relationship.

SUMMARY

This chapter has presented some general approaches to the long-term marital treatment of an eating-disordered couple, incuding suggestions for a therapeutic stance that allows the therapist to develop a trustworthy treatment relationship with the couple and to attend to the shame-based, insecure pattern of relating that maintains the eating disorder as a viable symptom. It also highlighted and explored some of the problems and crises that develop during various phases of treatment.

7

Empirical Studies of Couple Functioning

This chapter reviews results from our research program into the quality of marital interaction among married patients with eating disorders. Based primarily in the Eating Disorders Day Hospital at The Toronto Hospital, our investigations into marital quality are one part of our larger research interest in familial factors in eating disorders.

There are few empirical studies of marital functioning in this patient group. Aside from the work of Van den Broucke and Vandereycken (1989,a,b,c), reviewed in Chapter 2, we are not aware of any other such studies.

DESCRIPTION OF THE RESEARCH PROGRAM

Goals

The goals of our program are to investigate the nature of the marital interaction in eating disorders, with a particular focus on the effect of active symptomatology on the quality of marital satisfaction and on the short- and long-term courses of such marriages after recovery. Subsidiary areas of interest include comparing marital interactional patterns with those observed in the patients' families of origin and comparing the quality of marital interaction in eating disorders with that in other psychiatric conditions. Finally, we are keenly interested in the development of new family measures and the refinement of existing measures.

The Day Hospital Program provides an ideal setting in which to pursue these goals. Family involvement, both of families of origin and current families, is strongly encouraged and is the norm. We encourage this involvement of families of origin despite the fact that the program treats only adults. Clinical and research assessments are carried out at both admission and discharge, and also at two years posttreatment. Family therapy is often provided by a therapeutic team. The integration of our family research program into the larger clinical outcome research program at the Day Hospital allows for access not only to a wide variety of information on eating-disorder symptoms, but also to many indices of psychological functioning on the part of the identified patients. Close coordination with other clinical services in the hospital provides an opportunity to gather information on comparative samples.

Measures

The Process Model of Family Functioning and the Family Assessment Measure (FAM)

The Process Model of Family Functioning (PM) (Steinhauer et al., 1984) has its origins in the Family Categories Schema (Epstein, Rakoff, & Sigal, 1968). Drawing on these descriptions of "universal" dimensions of family functioning, the PM differs from these earlier models in several ways. First, it is a more process-oriented model, allowing for the evaluation of strengths in family functioning as well as of problem areas. Second, it is a theory of family functioning that is not derived from a theory of family intervention. Third, it contains a means of evaluating specific hypotheses, the Family Assessment Measure (FAM) (Skinner et al., 1983).

The FAM has items with a four-point, forced-choice format. It is a self-report instrument that consists of three scales. The General Scale focuses on how an individual in the family views the family as a whole. In addition to items relating to the seven dimensions of the PM, the

General Scale contains two response-style subscales, social desirability and defensiveness.

The Self-Rating Scale addresses how an individual views his or her own functioning within the family. The Dyadic Scale assesses specific relationship dyads within the family.

The FAM is administered in the following fashion. Each family member is provided with a General and a Self-Rating Scale, and enough copies of the Dyadic Scale to rate relevant dyadic relationships. What this produces is a family of General and Self-Rating Scale scores, one for each family member, and smaller groups of Dyadic Scale ratings, one group for each family member. Table 7.1 presents the dimensions of the FAM.

The Waring Intimacy Questionnaire

The 90-item, true–false Waring Intimacy Questionnaire (WIQ) was developed specifically to measure one component of marital adjustment, that of intimacy. Its development is described in detail elsewhere (Waring & Reddon, 1983). In addition to providing a total intimacy

TABLE 7.1.
Dimensions of the Process Model of Family Functioning

Dimension Name	*Concept Assessed*
Task accomplishment	Ability to perform basic tasks of family life; problem-solving ability
Role performance	Flexibility of role allocation; identification of idiosyncratic roles
Communication	Clarity; directness
Affective expression	Range, intensity, and timing of expression of affect
Involvement	Degree, quality, and nature of involvement
Control	Regulation of behavior; maintenance and adaptibility
Values and norms	Consistency of stated beliefs; congruency of explicit and implicit ideals
Response bias subscales (General Scale only)	
Social desirability	Tendency to respond in a favorable fashion
Defensiveness	Tendency to minimize problems

score as an estimate of the degree of marital intimacy in a particular couple, the WIQ produces scores evaluating eight critical aspects of marital intimacy. *Conflict resolution* assesses the couple's ability to identify and resolve conflicts as they arise. *Affection* addresses the couple's ability to demonstrate feelings of emotional closeness. *Cohesion* evaluates the couple's degree of commitment to the marriage, and *sexuality* identifies the degree to which sexual needs are expressed and fulfilled in the relationship. *Identity* focuses on issues of self-esteem and self-confidence, while *compatibility* examines the couple's ability to engage in shared activities together. *Autonomy* assesses active family-of-origin issues, while *expressiveness* addresses the extent to which couples can share their beliefs and feelings with each other. Finally, response bias is assessed via a subset of items that identify socially desirable responses.

Administration

The measures are administered as a clinical intervention at admission and at discharge. Most couples will complete them by the end of the first week of treatment, and within two weeks of discharge. While every effort is made to encourage couples to complete the measures, this is, of course, voluntary.

Efficacy of Day Hospital Treatment

The efficacy of the treatment offered in the setting of the Day Hospital has been extensively documented (Piran & Kaplan, 1990). Briefly, after 10 to 12 weeks of treatment, over 80% of patients previously suffering from BN no longer met the diagnostic criteria for the disorder: over 50 % were totally abstinent from bingeing and purging during the month prior to discharge. Our results with patients suffering from AN and AN/BN were not as good, with about 60% moderately or markedly improved. Results presented on couples at discharge should be viewed in this light, that is, in the light of significant reductions in symptom levels. Some of us have previously reported marked improvements in the ratings of family functioning that accompany improvements in eating symptomatology (Woodside et al., submitted for publication).

SUMMARY OF RESEARCH RESULTS

Demographics and Sample Description

Table 7.2 presents basic demographic and diagnostic information on the portion of our sample of married patients for whom we have at least some psychometric data. Throughout the chapter, the number of cases for each analysis will vary slightly, as data are missing in some cases for various of reasons. First, not all couples will complete the questionnaires at admission and discharge. This includes situations in which the patient was discharged prematurely, the spouse lived far enough away that there was minimal marital involvement, or one or both members of the couple simply refused. The use of the WIQ, as well, only started partway through the process of data collection. Approximately 50% of our patients suffer from BN alone, 20% from AN alone, and 20% from AN and BN concurrently. A few patients do not qualify for a DSM-III-R diagnosis of either AN or BN (for example, a patient who vomits all food eaten but does not binge or have a very low weight). Most members of our sample are legally married; all the common-law relationships

TABLE 7.2.
Demographic and Descriptive Data on
Married Patients Admitted to the DHP

Diagnoses:	Anorexia nervosa	7 (15.9%)
	Anorexia nervosa and bulimia	9 (20.5%)
	Bulimia nervosa	33 (52.3%)
	Eating disorder NOS	5 (11.4%)
Age:		29.4 ± 7.52 years
Duration of marriage:		7.8 ± 8.5 years

included have lasted more than two years, and many have endured for decades. The average age of our married patients is just under 30 years, compared with an average age of our Day Hospital population of about 25 years. The average duration of the marriages is 7.8 ± 8.5 years.

Table 7.3 presents some basic symptom data at admission and at discharge for married patients with BN. It will be noted that there was a significant reduction in the level of these symptoms between admission and discharge.

Statistical Analysis

Analyses were performed considering the seven dimensions of each FAM scale and the dimensions of the WIQ as being families of related variables; thus most analyses were multivariate analyses of variance (MANOVAs). For comparisons at different times (for example, before and after the Day Hospital Progam), a repeated-measures design was employed—a technique that results in a smaller number of cases for some analyses, but one that, we feel, is a more rigorous methodology. Wherever possible, we have included all the data we collected. Because of the large numbers of MANOVAs performed, we have grouped the analyses into four parts: spouse–patient comparisons, admission–discharge comparisons, comparisons with the ratings of the family of origin, and the WIQ analyses. For WIQ analyses, a significance level for main effects thus was set at 0.025 (four MANOVAs); for FAM admission–discharge analyses, at 0.025 (four MANOVAs); for comparisons with the family of origin at 0.025 (four MANOVAs); and for comparisons concerning the effect of ultimate clinical outcome status,

TABLE 7.3.
Symptom Levels at Admission and
Discharge ($n = 44$)

	Admission	Discharge
Binges	26.18/week	0.72/week
Vomiting episodes	56.21/week	1.00/week

Note: Patients with AN alone ($n = 7$, 15.9%) have no binge episodes.

0.016 (six MANOVAs). Analyses of demographic information were carried out by *t*-test or chi-squared analysis, depending on the nature of the data. Finally, it should be noted that no distinction was made within eating disorders according to diagnostic group (i.e., AN compared with BN) owing to the relatively small number of subjects assessed.

Marital Typology at Admission

Waring Intimacy Questionnaire Results

Tables 7.4 and 7.5 present WIQ scores for patients and spouses at admission and at discharge. These scores are presented graphically in Figure 7.1. It can be seen that ratings by patients are generally less favorable at admission as compared with ratings by spouses, with scores on the identity subscale (self-esteem) and the total intimacy score being very low (less favorable), and scores on several other dimensions also being significantly less favorable (cohesion, compatibility, autonomy, expressivity). Differences at posttreatment are slightly smaller, with

TABLE 7.4.
WIQ Scores for Patients at Admission and Discharge

WIQ Dimensions	Patient—Admission n = 20	Patient—Discharge n = 15
Conflict resolution	4.8 ± 3.3	6.4 ± 2.4
Affection	5.9 ± 2.4	6.3 ± 2.1
Cohesion	5.9 ± 2.2	6.1 ± 2.5
Sexuality	5.1 ± 1.8	5.4 ± 2.3
Identity	2.6 ± 2.3	4.1 ± 2.9
Compatibility	6.2 ± 2.3	7.0 ± 2.7
Autonomy	6.1 ± 1.8	5.5 ± 2.4
Expressivity	6.7 ± 2.4	8.1 ± 1.4
Social desirability	3.0 ± 3.2	3.8 ± 2.6
Total intimacy	20.4 ± 6.6	24.4 ± 7.1

Notes:
1. Num:bers of subjects represent all data available where both patients and spouses completed the questionnaire at admission or discharge.
2. Effect for time: $p < 0.001$. Cohesion, identity, expressivity, significant at the $p < 0.05$ level on univariate testing.
3. Social desirability, total intimacy signficant at $p < 0.05$.

TABLE 7.5.
WIQ Scores for Spouses at Admission and Discharge

WIQ Dimensions	*Spouse—Admission* $n = 20$	*Spouse—Discharge* $n = 15$
Conflict resolution	5.3 ± 3.0	6.9 ± 3.1
Affection	7.7 ± 1.7	7.4 ± 1.8
Cohesion	7.8 ± 1.3	7.9 ± 2.0
Sexuality	6.1 ± 1.3	6.3 ± 2.0
Identity	7.7 ± 2.4	9.0 ± 1.7
Compatibility	6.5 ± 1.8	6.9 ± 1.6
Autonomy	7.0 ± 2.3	7.0 ± 2.6
Expressivity	7.5 ± 2.0	7.6 ± 1.5
Social desirability	3.4 ± 3.4	3.4 ± 3.4
Total intimacy	29.8 ± 4.4	30.7 ± 5.4

Notes:
1. Numbers of subjects represent all data available where both patients and spouses completed the questionnaire at admission or discharge.
2. Effect for time: $p < 0.001$. Conflict resolution, cohesion, affection, identity, and expressivity significant at the $p < 0.05$ level on univariate testing.
3. Total intimacy significant at $p < 0.001$.

both patients and spouses showing statistically significant changes in ratings over the course of hospitalization. While most of the changes on individual dimensions are improvements, a few ratings are seen to be worse (patients—cohesion, autonomy, social desirability; spouses—affection, expressivity), although the differences are very small. Significantly, ratings on the social desirability dimension were well

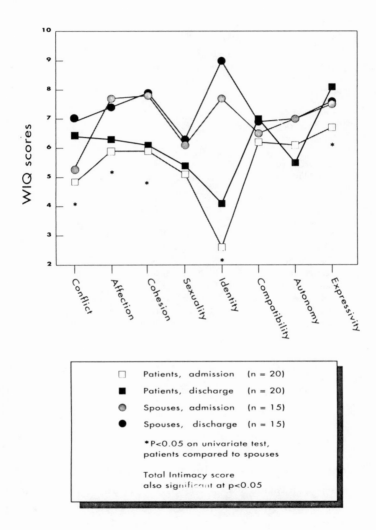

Figure 7.1. WIQ Scores for Patients and Spouses at Admission and Discharge

TABLE 7.6.
Effect of Ultimate Clinical Status at
Discharge on WIQ Scores at Admission

Main Effects		p	
Outcome		0.145	
Rater (patient/spouse)		0.001	
Interaction		0.035	

Univariate Tests		p	
WIQ Dimensions	Outcome	Rater	Interaction
Conflict resolution	0.287	0.117	0.737
Affection	0.977	0.184	0.666
Cohesion	0.064	0.001	0.130
Sexuality	0.768	0.256	0.532
Identity	0.073	0.001	0.215
Compatibility	0.600	0.004	0.865
Autonomy	0.579	0.001	1.000
Expressivity	0.587	0.046	0.513
Social desirability	0.259	0.489	0.880
Total intimacy	0.647	0.001	0.230

Note: $n = 12$ for good outcome, $n = 8$ for poor outcome.

within the normal range as described by Waring (1985).

One interesting question was whether the patient's ultimate clinical status at discharge might, in some way, affect either before- or after-treatment marital ratings. Could patients with better outcome have reduced levels of marital distress either at admission or at discharge? Tables 7.6 and 7.7 present the significance levels for main effects and

TABLE 7.7.
Effect of Ultimate Clinical Status at
Discharge on WIQ Scores at Discharge

Main Effects	p
Outcome	0.145
Rater (patient/spouse)	0.001
Interaction	0.035

Univariate Tests (main effect of rater)

	p
WIQ Dimensions	
Conflict resolution	1.000
Affection	0.288
Cohesion	0.003
Sexuality	0.001
Identity	0.001
Compatibility	0.830
Autonomy	0.034
Expressivity	0.002
Social desirability	0.145
Total intimacy	0.001

Notes:
1. $n = 12$ for good outcome, n = 8 for poor outcome.
2. Univariate tests for main effect of outcome, group and for the interaction effect are not presented as those main effects are not significant.

univariate tests at admission and discharge for this comparison. While there is no main effect for outcome group on ratings either by patients or by spouses, at either admission or discharge, there is a highly significant effect of who is doing the ratings (patient or spouse) at both times and a trend toward an interaction effect at admission. Figure 7.2 presents these data in graphic form, suggesting that this trend toward significance for an interaction effect might relate to a tendency of patients with ultimately poor clinical outcome to rate marital satisfaction as *higher* relative to other patients and the two groups of spouses at admission.

Family Assessment Measure Ratings of the Marriage

Table 7.8 presents significance levels for main effects comparing patient ratings with spousal ratings at admission and at discharge. Table 7.9 presents significance levels for comparisons of spousal and patient scores from admission to discharge. Figures 7.3 through 7.5 present these data in graphical form.

At admission, there are no significant differences between spouse and patient ratings on any of the three FAM scales (General, Self-Rating, and Dyadic). At discharge, there is a weak trend ($p = .076$ on Table 7.8) toward a difference on the General Scale, with no clear pattern of scores. There are no differences on the Self-Rating Scale or on the Dyadic Scale at discharge. Patients show a trend toward improved ratings over the course of the hospitalization on the General Scale ($p = 0.055$) and the Self-Rating Scale ($p = 0.020$). Spouses show a weak trend toward improved ratings on the General Scale ($p = 0.094$) and a significant improvement on the Self-Rating Scale ($p = 0.002$), with no changes on the Dyadic Scale.

As was done with WIQ scores, an analysis was performed examining whether ultimate clinical outcome at discharge had any effect on FAM scores at either admission or discharge. There was no effect of outcome on any scale either at admission or at discharge for patients and spouses.

Comparisons with Ratings of Family of Origin

Comparisons were made examining how patients' ratings of their own marital situations corresponded to patients' rating of their own families of origin, both at admission and at discharge. On the General Scale, there was no difference between marital and family-of-origin rat-

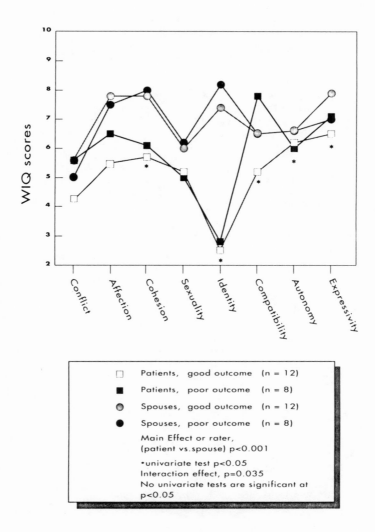

Figure 7.2. WIQ Scores for Patients and Spouses, According to Ultimate Clinical Outcome

TABLE 7.8.
FAM Ratings by Patients and Spouses—
Main Effect of Rater at Admission and
Discharge for Each FAM Scale

Admission *FAM scale*	*p*
General Scale ($n = 28$)	0.306
Self-Rating Scale ($n = 29$)	0.514
Dyadic Scale ($n = 28$)	0.385
Discharge *FAM Scale*	*p*
General Scale ($n = 24$)	0.076
Self-Rating Scale ($n = 24$)	0.437
Dyadic Scale ($n = 24$)	0.699

Note: Dyadic comparisons are patient rates spouse compared with spouse rates patient.

TABLE 7.9.
FAM Ratings by Patients and
Spouses—Main Effect of Time
Between Admission and Discharge
for Each FAM Scale

Admission *FAM Scale*	*p*	
	Patients	Spouses
General Scale ($n = 28$)	0.055	0.094
Self-Rating Scale ($n = 29$)	0.020	0.002
Dyadic Scale ($n = 28$)	0.226	0.796

Notes: Dyadic comparisons are patient rates spouse compared with spouse rates patient.

Univariate tests significant at the $p < 0.05$ level are shown in Figures 7.3–7.5.

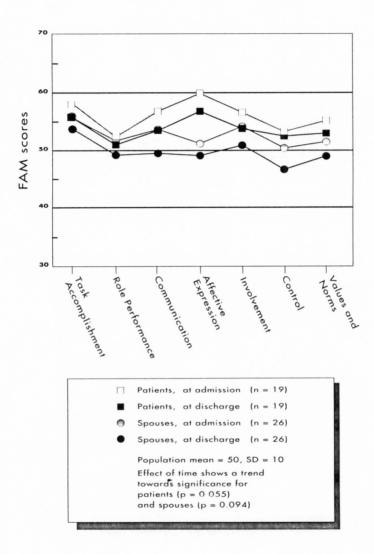

Figure 7.3. FAM General Scale Scores, Patients and Spouses, at Admission and Discharge

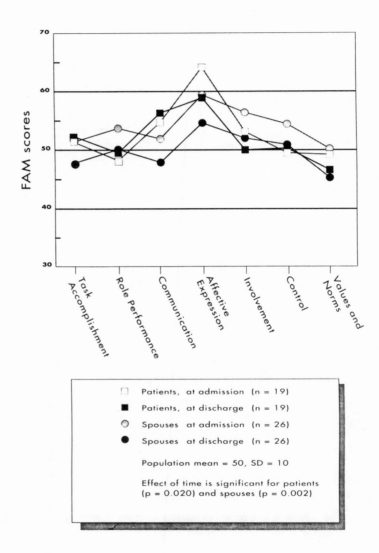

Figure 7.4. FAM Self-Rating Scores, Patients and Spouses, at Admission and Discharge

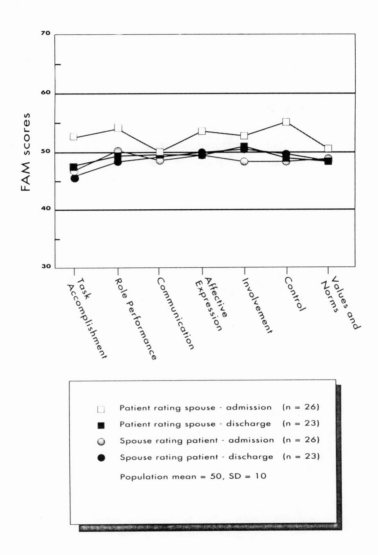

Figure 7.5. FAM Dyadic Scale Scores, Patients and Spouses, at Admission and Discharge

ings. However, on the Self-Rating Scale, patients rated their own functioning in their own marriage much more positively than they rated
their own functioning in their families of origin ($p = 0.009$). This was
true at both admission and discharge ($p = 0.018$). There was a significant interaction effect ($p = 0.014$), suggesting in this case that ratings
of family of origin were improving at a greater rate than were ratings
of the marriage. These data are presented in Table 7.10 and Figures
7.6.and 7.7. When Dyadic Scale ratings done by patients on their own
mothers, fathers, and spouses were compared at admission, there was
a weak trend ($p = 0.061$) for patients' ratings of their own fathers to be
slightly less favorable than their ratings of their own mothers or
spouses. This was no longer the case at discharge, when there were no
differences in patients' ratings of these three individuals. These data are
presented graphically in Figure 7.8.

TABLE 7.10.
**FAM Ratings by Patients—Ratings of Current Family Compared
with Ratings of Family of Origin at Admission and Discharge**

Main Effects

FAM Scale	Time	Family	Interaction
Interaction			
General Scale ($n = 17$)	0.607	0.183	0.081
Self-Rating Scale ($n = 17$)	0.018	0.009	0.014

	Target (mother, father, spouse)		
Dyadic Scale-pre ($n = 23$)	0.061		
Dyadic Scale-post ($n = 13$)	0.612		

Univariate Tests for the Self-Rating Scale ($n = 17$)

FAM Dimension	Time	Family	Interaction
Task accomplished	0.032	0.001	0.225
Role performance	0.042	0.218	0.113
Communication	0.227	0.880	0.001
Affective expression	0.044	0.534	0.136
Involvement	0.794	0.064	0.406
Control	0.519	0.106	0.140
Values and Norms	0.001	0.065	0.067

Note: Dyadic Scale ratings compare patient ratings of spouses with patient ratings of mothers and fathers; "target" refers to the target of the *patient's* rating.

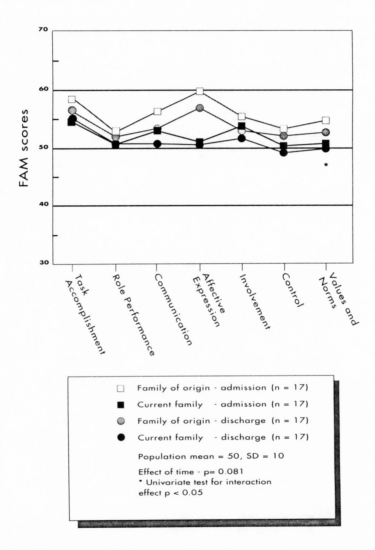

Figure 7.6. FAM General Scale Ratings—Patients Rating Family of Origin and Current Family at Admission and Discharge

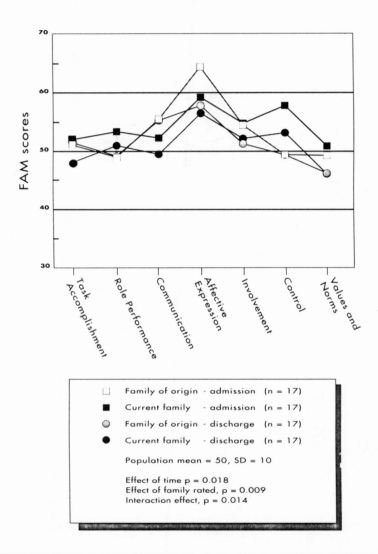

Figure 7.7. FAM Self-Rating Scale Ratings—Patients Rating Family of Origin and Current Family, at Admission and Discharge

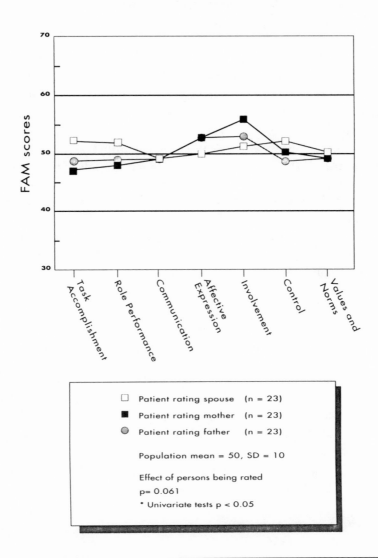

Figure 7.8. Dyadic Scale Ratings—Patients Rating Spouses, Mothers and Fathers at Admission

Comparisons with Ratings of Marital Functioning by Patients with Anxiety Disorders

Ratings of marital functioning by patients with eating disorders have not previously been compared with ratings of marital quality by individuals with other major psychiatric illnesses. A sample of patients was recruited from the Anxiety Disorders Clinic at The Toronto General Hospital (now The Toronto General Division of The Toronto Hospital), all of whom were asked to rate either their families of origin or their marriages using the General and Self-Rating Scales of the FAM. Ratings of marriages produced by patients with anxiety disorders were then compared with ratings by a subsample of our married patients, in the fashion described above. There were no significant differences between ratings by these two groups, regardless of whether their families of origin or their marriages were being rated. These findings are presented graphically in Figures 7.9 and 7.10.

Summary of Findings

WIQ Ratings

Patients consistently rate their marriage less favorably than do their spouses. While these differences are diminished after intensive Day hospitalization, they are still significantly different. Several ratings by patients and spouses show a trend toward increased difficulty at the end of treatment, but these changes are very small. There is no evidence of excessive social desirability in the responses of either patients or spouses. Finally, patients with poorer ultimate clinical outcome may rate marital satisfaction more positively at admission.

FAM Ratings of the Marriage

There were no significant differences in ratings by patients or their spouses on any of the FAM scales. Ultimate clinical outcome at discharge did not affect FAM ratings at any point, or by either rater. There

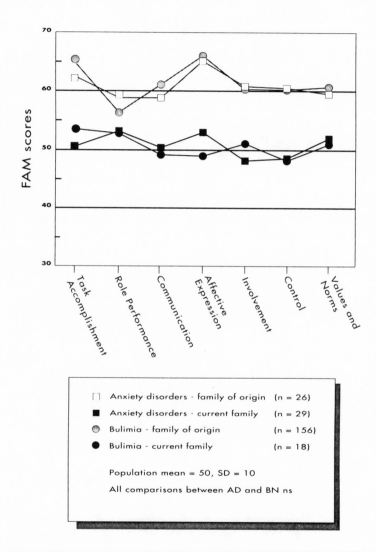

Figure 7.9. FAM General Scale Ratings—Comparing Families of Origin and Current Families with Anxiety and Eating Disorders

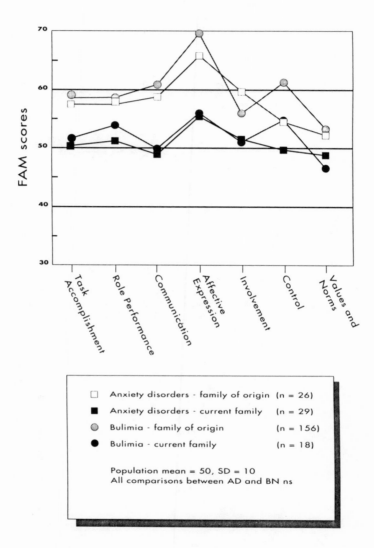

Figure 7.10. FAM Self-Rating Scale Ratings—Comparing Families of Origin and Current Families for Patients with Anxiety and Eating Disorders

is no evidence of excessive social desirability or defensiveness on the part of either the patient or spouse at any time.

Comparison of FAM Ratings of the Marriage and of the Patient's Family of Origin

At admission to the hospital, patients' ratings of their families of origin indicated greater difficulties in functioning than did their ratings of their marriages on the Self-Rating Scale. Despite improvements in these ratings after treatment, these differences still persist at discharge. There is a weak trend at admission for patients to rate their relationships with their fathers as less favorable than their relationships with their mothers or spouses. This is not the case at discharge. There is no evidence of excessive social desirability or defensiveness on the part of either the patient or her parents at any time, and thus there is no evidence that these ratings of the family of origin are related to denial of difficulty.

Comparison of FAM Ratings of Patients with Anxiety Disorders and with Eating Disorders

There were no significant differences in these ratings.

CLINICAL SIGNIFICANCE OF THESE FINDINGS

Quality of Marriage in Patients with Eating Disorders

There is clear evidence from WIQ data that these patients experience some marital discord. That their view is not entirely shared by their spouses does not necessarily mean that one view is correct and one is incorrect; the very existence of large discrepancies in points of view is a problem in itself. Patients have extremely low scores on the dimension of identity. This perhaps should not be surprising, since the dimension of identity is probably closely related to the concept of self-esteem, which is known to be a problem for patients with eating disorders. Two other dimensions on which patients score much more in the direction of the problem range are affection (nonsexual expression of caring) and cohesion (commitment to the relationship). The total intimacy scores also are different by a clinically significant degree.

Results from FAM data, on the other hand, provide no clear evidence of marital discord, in terms either of absolute scores or of differences between patients and spouses. This may in part relate to the development of the FAM as a tool primarily employed in assessing larger family units; however, one would have expected some ability to assess the marital dyad via the Dyadic Scale of the FAM.

Changes Over Time

While WIQ and FAM scores indicate clear changes in the direction of more favorable ratings by patients at discharge as compared with admission, this is not the case for spouses. Resolving these conflicting results may be made easier by noting that patients' WIQ scores significantly improve over the course of hospitalization, which is associated with marked symptom reduction for most patients. As some of us have observed (Woodside et al., submitted for publication), patients' ratings of their families of origin using the FAM show a similar trend over the course of the DHP—that is, less favorable ratings by patients at admission and much more normal ratings by discharge. The magnitude of the changes in WIQ scores on the part of patients between admission and discharge is fairly large, and, in general, they indicate improvement. As is the case with FAM ratings of parents in families of origin (Woodside et al., submitted for publication), spousal scores remain consistent over this same time course. Thus the net effect is one of increasing congruence as symptoms are removed.

Possible Effects of Patient Views of Family of Origin

Patients view their families of origin as more troubling and in a less favorable light than their marriages, as measured by the FAM. However, this is statistically significant only for the Self-Rating Scale and the Patient Rates Father Dyadic Scale. While the Self-Rating Scale ratings and marital ratings show no change at discharge, significant improvement is seen in the ratings of families of origin. It is conceivable that this pattern of ratings reflects the patients' tendency to ascribe difficulties in the marriage to their families of origin; this could be related to the shame-bound nature of these families, as hypothesized in Chapter 3, and the improvements to an increased sense of security derived from a treatment experience that acts to reduce feelings of shame in concert with reduced eating symptoms. In any event, if this were true, one might well expect to see a reversal in the pattern of ratings (ratings of spouses becoming worse than ratings of parents) as symptoms were removed and the "truth" revealed. But, as has been described, this does not appear to occur. Less favorable ratings on the Self-Rating Scale could represent increased levels of shame in the patients, as discussed in Chapter 3; however, the hypothesized accompanying shame on the part of the families of origin may not be present. It is possible that the low scores on the WIQ dimension of identity also relate to the same issue of shame-proneness in this clinical group.

Significance of Comparison with Anxiety Disorder Patients

The lack of any difference between the ratings of these two clinical groups is fascinating. Figures 7.9 and 7.10 show that the scores are virtually identical. This speaks very strongly to a significant effect on ratings of family of origin that could be caused by a general illness, rather than by a diagnosis-specific family pathology. The combination of these observations and the changes noted over the course of symptom removal presents, in our opinion, a fairly compelling case for the existence of such a nonspecific, illness effect. It does not, however, explain the discrepancy between WIQ and FAM results noted above.

Clinical Outcome

In Chapter 2, we noted that many writers were pessimistic about the outcome of married patients (Crisp, 1977; Crisp et al., 1977; Hsu et al., 1979; Morgan & Russell, 1975; Andersen, 1985; Dally, 1984; Russell, 1979; Van den Broucke & Vandereycken, 1989b). In our own series, 12 out of 20 (60%) had good clinical outcome at the conclusion of hospitalization. That is, if bulimic, they did not binge or purge during the four weeks prior to discharge; if anorexic, they exceeded 90% of chart average weight; and if suffering from both anorexia and bulimia, they met both criteria. This compares favorably to the overall rates of good outcome, 55% for BN and 45% for AN.

Effect of These Findings on the Marital Assessment of Patients with Eating Disorders

We recommend that great care be taken in the assessment of these marriages. In particular, we suggest strongly that therapists avoid making global assumptions about pathology in these marriages, and recognize that abnormal eating itself is likely to have a very disruptive effect on the quality of any marriage. This does not preclude making hypotheses about factors in the marriage that might have been implicated in the development of the eating disorder, but these should be considered to be only hypotheses until the identified patient's eating is more stable and a more complete assessment can be performed. It is important to remember that many married eating-disordered patients were ill long before the initiation of their marital relationship.

It is, however, also very important to identify marital factors that may be perpetuating the eating disorder. A decision about the degree of marital pathology that such perpetuating factors indicate may also be best left until eating is more normal; our experience has been that they can fade away as the abnormal eating abates. In other cases, such factors as the spouse's having based the decision to marry on the patient's viewed helplessness and need for nurturance can be a major obstacle not only to recovery, but also to the health of the marriage later on.

Effect on Treatment Recommendations

Even if a definitive formulation of the marriage must await resolution of abnormal eating, it is very helpful to provide educational support to spouses. In fact, the manner in which such psychoeducation is received will often prove to be illuminating. Clearly, the initial focus of couple treatment in this clinical group must be to facilitate the normalization of the identified patient's eating; treatment in which this is not a focus is unlikely to be mutative, and may be actively harmful. A careful reassessment at the time of the resolution of eating symptoms is obviously indicated.

SUMMARY

This chapter has reviewed empirical data related to the quality of the marriages of eating-disordered patients, changes in the marriage over the course of the resolution of symptoms, and how patients' ratings of their own marriages compare with their ratings of their families of origin and with similar ratings by patients with anxiety disorders. Patients generally rate their marriages and their families of origin less favorably than do their spouses or their parents, and there are no differences between such ratings, whether provided by patients with eating disorders or by patients with anxiety disorders.

8

Eating-Disordered Patients as Parents

Chapter 2 reviewed the literature on parenting by patients with eating disorders, noting that there has been a relative dearth of observations on this topic. Given the marked social, emotional, and physical impairment that follows the development of an eating disorder, it is important that the subject be addressed.

Briefly, the review in Chapter 2 suggests that an active eating disorder may have some effect on the ability to parent. The discussion here, both clinical and theoretical in nature, is based on our observations of 30 patients, who are the parents of over 50 children and who were admitted to the Day Hospital Program at The Toronto Hospital over the past six years. As is the case with any sample derived from a specialized treatment clinic, it must be assumed a priori that the sample is biased, probably toward more difficult situations, and that it is thus not likely to be representative of the entire population of patients with eating disorders who are also parents. The value of using this sample is that one or more of the authors has had the opportunity to work with each of the parents intensively, as well as to observe their children first hand.

This chapter describes a tentative "family life cycle" of parenting difficulties found in each developmental stage, presents data on the quality of the patients' marriages, and comments on how this formulation might affect decisions about clinical management. The life cycle stages borrow some terms from specific formulations of child development;

TABLE 8.1.
The Parenting Life Cycle

Parenting Stage	Active Issues	Children's Behavior
Parents of young children (up to age 5)	Establishment of basic pattern of parenting, including recruiting others to help/take over	Early awareness of parent's illness; primitive attempts to soothe parents
Parents of latency-age children (5–12 years)	Erosion of status quo and of established patterns; increased need for stability	Some children accept in more overt parentification, others may act out; early development of eating disorder possible in late latency age
Parents of teenage children	Need for stability on the part of the parent conflicts with need for individuation and autonomy on the part of the child	Children may continue parentified role or possibly act out, including developing eating disorders

however, we do this only for convenience, as there are no established terms to describe stages of parenting.

THE PARENTING LIFE CYCLE

Parents of Young Children

Parents of children five years old and younger are usually engaged in a struggle to establish a routine around parenting, while simultaneously attempting to cope with eating-disorder symptoms. This routine can include very basic tasks, such as meal preparation, and more abstract issues, such as who will be responsible for which parts of the child's education. Depending on the resources of the parents, the establishment of such a routine may involve recruiting additional help, often in the form of the family of origin. While necessary, and thus adaptive, this strategy can expose some parents to the reactivation of earlier unresolved conflicts around issues of separation and autonomy, and may set the stage for later impairments of marital intimacy. Children who are going through their own developmental sequence during this parenting stage tend to become increasingly aware of the ill parent's behavior, and will engage in attempts to soothe the affected parent in a fashion consistent with their own developmental capacity.

A three-year-old son of a woman who was severely ill with BN continually promised his mother that he would be good if she would only stop vomiting.

Many of our parents who have only very young children do not report significant difficulties with the parenting role, but this may be so because of their lack of awareness of the child's behavior.

Harold was married and had one daughter, age two and a half. He professed to be fond of his daughter, but generally was absent, especially at meals.

For other patients, the other parent or other family had taken over much of the work of parenting the child.

Grace (described in Chapter 4) had severe AN and BN, complicated by chronic incapacitating depression that required long hospitalizations. During these periods, her husband and his family shared the work of caring for the child.

Generally, during this stage of parenting, resources within the marriage or extended family are required to fill in for the effectively absent parent. When this happens, the assessment of parenting effectiveness by the parents themselves is problematic. What may appear to be a normal family situation may in fact represent a system that is utilizing the parenting skills of a nanny, mother, or other caregiver, and may itself be unable to cope with even the basic maintenance of the child. Additional stresses, such as older children, children with greater demands, or more children, may overload such a system. It must be emphasized that the recruitment of additional resources is an adaptive move on the part of such families. The difficulty is that this adaptation is fragile, and later stresses, such as deaths or other illnesses, often leave these systems very vulnerable. Children also may be recruited, and begin to develop a parentified stance.

Doris who sufferred from BN, had coped reasonably well with her son, age three, until recently. She had separated from her sexually abusive husband about a year previously, and had been struggling to finish her university education while acting as a single parent. Both of her parents were dead, and her only remaining immediate family was a sister, who lived in a different city. Much to her surprise, she learned that her son had been aware of her vomiting since he was about two and a half. By the time she was admitted to the DHP, he was trying to prevent her from going into the bathroom alone and he was refusing to eat, saying that he hoped that if he did not eat, his mother would not have to vomit. Overwhelmed by these problems and devoid of any significant support, the patient felt that her only alternative was to give over the care of the child to her husband.

Probably the most significant factors protective of both the child and the patient's relationship with the child during this stage are a stable marital relationship and the availability of other resources to support the parent who has an active eating disorder. Unfortunately, as described earlier, many cases of later-onset AN may be related to marital dissatisfaction, and, in any case, the effect of a chronic illness may markedly impair marital relationships. An additional complicating factor in the group with older onset may be the reduced availability of family resources due to the aging and illness of grandparents.

Mary (described in Chapter 4) had developed AN at age 32 in the setting of an unhappy marriage of 13 years' duration. Unable to concentrate on negotiating an appropriate separation agreement owing to her extreme starvation, she allowed herself to agree that the children could not be moved more than 10 miles from their location at the time. Unfortunately, she herself was forced to move to another city because of her job, and thus had to leave the care of the children to her husband. She considered returning to the city in which the children lived, but realized that she would require considerable support if she were to regain custody of the children. Her parents, both over 70, were physically ill and unable to commit to providing her with such help.

Latency-Age children

Issues for parents of children ages five through 12 tend to be a function of the age of the child and the family's circumstances. For younger children, this may be the time when additional stressors, in the form of more children, parental marital distress, or the death or illness of a grandparent begin to erode a fragile status quo. Many children in such situations will become model children, in an effort to reduce family stress. Many of these efforts are related in some way to the eating disorder. Should increasing stresses on the family result in marital discord, it is easy for children to become parentified and actively triangulated into the marriage, usually allied with the identified patient. When this occurs, the identification can produce eating-disorder symptoms toward the end of the latency-age period. Alternatively, such symptoms can arise as acting-out or internal self-soothing behaviors.

Mary (described earlier) had two children, a son eight years of age and a daughter aged 12. During her stay in the hospital, on Mother's Day, her daughter gave her a hand-made card that duplicated the eating diary that all the patients fill out, down to the visual analog scales for feelings.

Eunice, a 35-year-old woman, had a son aged 16; she had left her physically abusive, alcoholic husband when her son was six years old. She described the great help the son had been to her as a latency-age child, when he had done most of the shopping and cooking for the family.

As children move through the latency age, they move into the age of risk for becoming preoccupied with weight and shape themselves, or for becoming more actively involved in parental concerns. This can represent another way to become parentified, in these cases by the mechanism of identification.

Terry (described in Chapter 4) had two children, a son five years of age and a daughter seven years of age. The patient enforced strict dietary rules at home for her daughter, vowing that she "would never have to suffer what I've suffered." At one point, due to an unrelated illness, she became unable to enforce the diet, and her daughter promptly gained 10 pounds. A few months later, while profoundly depressed, the patient was horrified to discover that her daughter was hiding food in the hope that if her mother did not see her eating it, she would become less depressed.

Louise's 12-year-old daughter had finally gone to her father to communicate her distress when her mother was able to fit into her jeans.

Robert, a 31-year-old married man with BN, had two daughters, aged 12 and 4. His older daughter was very similar to her mother in appearance, and functioned as a pseudo-wife, preparing meals for her father and going on a diet at the same time that he was admitted for treatment.

Children of eating-disordered parents are particularly interesting at this age in a number of respects. First, despite almost universal protestations to the contrary on the part of the parents, the majority of the latency-age children we have encountered have been quite aware of their affected parent's unusual eating habits. Our sample is as yet too small to say whether female children are more aware of this behavior than male children. Second, despite this awareness, overt behavioral disturbance appears to be unusual in the latency age group; the most common reaction appears to be various forms of parentification, such as soothing the parent by preparing meals or by attuning to the parent (identification) in ways such as dieting. The former might well be a reaction to the increased stresses that are common in the family at this life-cycle stage, exacerbated by one important family member's being more or less covertly ill. The latter, however, is more likely to relate to the child's need to protect the affected parent.

Fiona, a 31-year-old separated woman, had a long history of AN and BN. She was mother of two boys, aged three and five years, and while her marital relationship had been bitter, her ex-husband continued to support her efforts to parent her children. The older boy presented as a powerful child who was very aware of his mother's symptoms. He would follow his mother around the apartment and invite her to join him and his brother for meals. She was able to provide them with balanced meals, but she would not eat with them, and she would usually binge on the leftovers after they had gone to bed. The children attended a lunch session and remarked how much they liked eating at "this restaurant"; they asked if they could come back and eat with their mother again.

Parents of Teenage Children

In our sample, the children of our patients have tended to take one of two paths at adolescence: toward a continuation of the perfectionistic, parentified role, or toward overt behavioral disturbances, such as truancy, drug or alcohol use, promiscuity, or difficulties with the law.

Eunice's son, the young boy referred to above, who was so helpful as a latency-age child, quickly became a major behavioral problem as he entered adolescence. By the age of 16, at the time of Eunice's admission, he had been charged with drug trafficking, and his girlfriend (who had an eating disorder) was concerned about pregnancy.

Georgia, a 53-year-old woman with BN, had three daughters, and acknowledged that she had an overly close relationship with her third daughter, who was still living at home at the age of 19. She was unsure that she would be able to allow her daughter to leave home and take up her own life.

Harriet, a 45-year-old woman who had AN and BN for many years, was mother to two daughters, aged 21 and 17 years, and grandmother to a newborn infant, the child of her younger daughter. She had suffered from AN for 20 years. She had married at the age of 20 to escape the physically and sexually abusive grandparental home in which she had been raised since the age of six, after her own parents had separated. Her marriage was characterized by extreme distance and aloofness between the spouses. Her parenting style was highly intrusive and demanding, and yet conflict avoidant. She was alternately critical and protective of her daughters, seldom allowing them to do things for themselves, preferring to "do it correctly myself." In the guise of helping her younger daughter, she took over the role of parenting her new grandchild; this served to undermine the daughter's already fragile self-confidence.

This younger child had behavioral problems in the form of sexual promiscuity and drug and alcohol use, and at the time of Harriet's admission, had just moved from a group home for adolescents into a small apartment with her newborn child. The older daughter was unwilling to leave home, and had recently invited her own boyfriend to live with her, together with Harriet and Harriet's husband.

Both daughters complained about their mother's intrusiveness, but also worried about her health. Although they presented a front of strength, they acknowledged significant fears about autonomy. Harriet's adoption of the role of caretaker allowed her to ignore her rather empty marriage, but also required the children to continue to present her with new worries to keep her distracted.

In the first case, the son's behavior might be viewed as a conflicted and self-destructive attempt to establish a sense of autonomy and to move out of the role of parent; if this were so, it was certainly having an effect. For children such as the daughter in the second case, their own needs to develop a sense of autonomy may be significantly delayed as they attempt carefully to negotiate some way out of their parentified role without distressing the parent excessively. This problem is fully developed in the third example, where both children made attempts but were unable to exit from this role.

Critical Inability to Perform the Role of Parent

While the above examples provide ample evidence that parenting can be impaired, in each case the parent with an eating disorder continued to function as best as possible under the circumstances. However, a very substantial group of patients are either effectively or totally unable to parent. This deficit may have mild effects in instances where the parenting is given over to a relative, but even this form of adaptation can lead to family and marital conflicts.

Ingrid was a 24-year-old woman who had been living in a common-law relationship for three years; the couple had a two-year-old son. She presented with a 10-year history of AN followed by BN. She had had a significant period of remission between late adolescence and the birth of her child; she relapsed almost immediately after he was born. Ingrid's parenting style was extremely inconsistent, and once her son was able to protest this, she began to view parenting as a problem for herself. Despite her partner's efforts to help, she found full-time parenting difficult, and eventually went to her mother for assistance. A pattern developed in which Ingrid's mother and stepfather would care for the child about half of the time. During a family meeting that included the child, it became evident how angry and in conflict all family members were about the situation. Both Ingrid and her mother wished to be identified as the primary caretaker of the child, but neither was able to take on this role on a full-time basis.

Joan, a 34-year-old divorced woman with BN and alcoholism, was raised in a very religious home and married at age 19 when she accidentally became pregnant. A second child was born two years later. Her eating disorder began in the context of her attempting to reconcile with her husband shortly after the birth of the second child. Joan initially had custody of the children, but voluntarily gave them up to their father and moved 2000 miles away to be closer to her own parents, citing her own inability to care for her children. At the time of her admission to the hospital, she had had no contact with her ex-husband and children for four years, and was fearful even of writing to them.

Karen, a 39-year-old woman with a long history of BN and alcoholism, left her husband and her two sons, ages four and six, because "I couldn't take care of myself, let alone them." She exchanges Christmas and birthday cards with her children, and sees them occasionally, but has had little to do with their care.

Lilly, a 41-year-old woman, had a decades-long history of AN and BN. She had given custody of twin children, a boy and a girl, to their father when they were quite young because she felt unable to care for them owing to the severity of her eating disorder. At the time of her admission, she had not had any contact with her children for 14 years.

Many patients with eating disorders have comorbid substance abuse; Karen and Lily (described above) both had very severe problems with alcohol, and this may have played a part in their eventual decisions to give up the care of their children. However, we feel it also emphasizes the delicate equilibrium in which these individuals function, where their role as parent may well depend on the good will of others. Such a situation will only perpetuate the eating disorder, as it will adversely affect the patient's self-esteem and increase the feeling of being out of control.

MARITAL QUALITY IN PATIENTS WHO ARE PARENTS

In the setting of the Day Hospital Program, as described above, we have been involved in the treatment of 70 patients who were currently married or had been married in the past. A number of these couples have been assessed with psychometric measures as described in Chapter 7.

The sample reviewed here consists of a subset of those married patients admitted to the program over the past six years. A total of 44 married patients with children were admitted, but psychometric data are not available in all cases, and we have chosen to use a repeated-measures design (including subjects only where both admission and discharge data are available) whenever possible to increase the rigor of the statistical analysis. Thus for example, couples for whom posttreatment ratings were not completed are not included in the analyses in this chapter.

Analyses were done using a multivariate analysis of variance (MAN-OVA), utilizing the dimensions of the WIQ and FAM as families of related variables. As mentioned above, a repeated-measures design was used wherever feasible. Analysis of demographic variables was performed using *t*-tests or chi-squared analyses as appropriate.

We compared rates of marital separation and divorce in our sample, for couples both with and without children. There was no difference in the rates of separation and divorce in the two groups ($p = .0.95$), the rates being identical (43% separated or divorced, 57% still married). The average duration of marriage for our divorced patients was 6.4 years, and for our separated patients, 4.2 years. The average duration of the marriages of our patients was 4.2 years for those without children and 12.88 years for those with children ($p = 0.008$). It is interesting to note that only about a third of the couples had children. We compared the ages of our married patients with and without children and found that those with children were quite a bit older, 36.8 years versus 27.4 years ($p = 0.003$). Of the patients who had been married and later were separated or divorced, those with children were also significantly older (40 years versus 30.5 years, $p = 0.10$). While the age difference between the two groups will account for some of the latter couples' lack of children, it may not reflect the whole story, given the relatively high mean age of the patients.

We have WIQ results (Waring & Reddon, 1983) for a subsample of our currently married patients. Table 8.2 displays these data for patients and spouses with and without children, while Figure 8.1 pre-

TABLE 8.2.
Waring Intimacy Questionnaire Scores

WIQ Subscales	Patients—with Children ($n = 11$)	Patients—No Children ($n = 15$)	Spouses—with Children ($n = 10$)	Spouses—No Children ($n = 15$)
Conflict	4.4 ± 3.2	5.1 ± 3.5	5.4 ± 1.8	5.4 ± 3.1
Affection	4.9 ± 2.3	6.4 ± 2.1	7.4 ± 1.2	7.6 ± 2.2
Cohesion	4.7 ± 1.8	7.3 ± 1.8	7.9 ± 1.3	7.7 ± 1.4
Sexuality	4.8 ± 1.9	4.7 ± 1.6	5.8 ± 1.4	5.5 ± 1.5
Identity	2.9 ± 2.8	2.1 ± 2.1	7.1 ± 2.5	7.4 ± 2.6
Communication	5.2 ± 2.4	6.5 ± 2.1	6.9 ± 1.4	5.7 ± 2.1
Autonomy	6.0 ± 1.9	5.9 ± 1.9	7.6 ± 2.2	7.0 ± 1.9
Expressivity	5.4 ± 2.5	7.4 ± 1.8	7.9 ± 1.7	7.2 ± 1.9
Social desirability	2.8 ± 2.8	3.8 ± 2.9	3.6 ± 3.1	4.6 ± 3.4
Total intimacy	17.9 ± 6.9	22.8 ± 5.4	28.2 ± 4.5	28.9 ± 6.2

Notes:
1. Main effect of having children: for patients, $p = 0.104$, cohesion and affective expression $p < 0.05$ on univariate testing; for spouses, $p = 0.410$.
2. Effect of having children, total intimacy score: patients, $p = 0.067$; spouses, $p = 0.735$.
3. Patients compared with spouses, total intimacy score, both groups combined: $p < 0.001$.

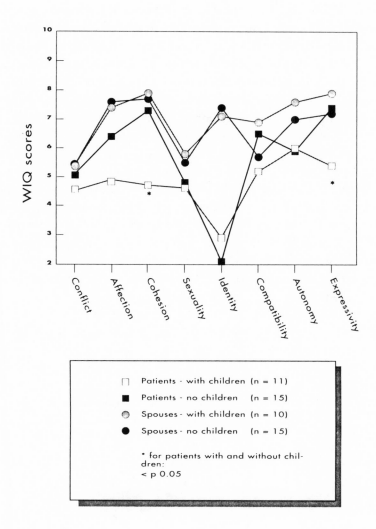

Figure 8.1. Waring Intimacy Questionnaire Scores, for Patients and Spouses, with and without Children

sents this data graphically. Ratings by patients who are parents show a trend toward being more problematic overall ($p = 0.104$), with only the dimensions of cohesion ($p = 0.001$) and expressivity ($p = 0.022$) being significantly worse for patients with children, and the total intimacy score showing a trend in the same direction ($p = 0.067$). Interestingly, spousal ratings of the marriage do not differ according to whether the couple does or does not have children.

Data are also available on a subset of our sample using the FAM (Skinner et al., 1983), as described in Chapter 7. Table 8.3 presents General Scale ratings by patients and spouses, and these data are presented graphically in Figure 8.2. These ratings show no effect of having children on ratings by patients ($p = 0.729$), but do show a trend toward such an effect for spouses ($p = 0.051$). However, none of the univariate tests for spouses are significant, and as Figure 8.2 demonstrates, there is no clear pattern to any differences in the scores on each dimension.

Table 8.4 provides similar data for Self-Rating Scale ratings. The data are also presented in graph form in Figure 8.3. In contrast to the General Scale, there is a weak trend for an effect of having children for patients ($p = 0.118$), with the dimensions of involvement and task accomplishment receiving more problematic ratings by patients with children. There is no effect of having children ($p = 0.460$) for spouses on the Self-Rating Scale.

TABLE 8.3.
General Scale Ratings for Patients and Spouses

FAM Dimensions	Patients—with Children ($n = 12$)	Patients—No Children ($n = 20$)	Spouses—with Children ($n = 11$)	Spouses—No Children ($n = 21$)
Task accomplished	60.5 ± 13.7	51.8 ± 10.1	52.1 ± 9.7	51.9 ± 9.7
Role performance	55.3 ± 14.1	48.4 ± 15.6	48.5 ± 9.6	47.1 ± 9.0
Communication	54.8 ± 13.5	47.4 ± 12.9	52.3 ± 8.7	48.6 ± 8.5
Affective expression	53.2 ± 15.0	50.6 ± 11.4	48.3 ± 9.2	53.6 ± 8.5
Involvement	56.6 ± 14.2	49.0 ± 12.1	52.9 ± 8.4	46.6 ± 9.6
Control	51.8 ± 11.0	47.0 ± 14.3	50.1 ± 8.3	49.3 ± 10.4
Values and norms	53.6 ± 9.8	48.6 ± 13.1	51.6 ± 8.1	46.3 ± 9.0

Note: Effect of having children: $p = 0.729$ for patients, $p = 0.051$ for spouses. No univariate tests are significant for spouses.

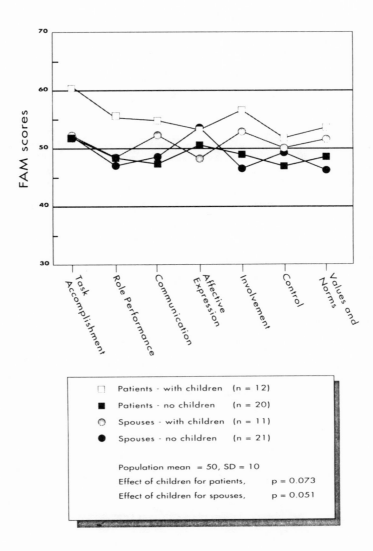

Figure 8.2. FAM General Scale, for Patients and Spouses, with and without Children

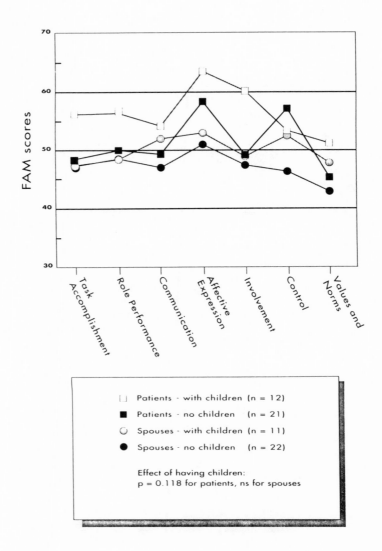

Figure 8.3. FAM Self-Rating Scale, for Patients and Spouses, with and without Children

TABLE 8.4.
Self-Rating Scale Ratings for Patients and Spouses

FAM Dimensions	Patients—with Children (n = 12)	Patients—No Children (n = 20)	Spouses—with Children (n = 11)	Spouses—No Children (n = 22)
Task accomplished	56.2 ± 11.4	48.5 ± 8.0	47.4 ± 10.6	47.3 ± 7.1
Role performance	56.4 ± 8.7	50.0 ± 13.8	48.4 ± 12.8	48.5 ± 10.9
Communication	54.2 ± 12.8	49.3 ± 10.6	52.0 ± 13.5	47.0 ± 12.3
Affective expression	63.5 ± 17.2	58.4 ± 14.0	53.0 ± 12.7	51.0 ± 8.8
Involvement	60.2 ± 11.6	49.2 ± 10.8	48.9 ± 9.0	47.4 ± 8.9
Control	53.4 ± 15.3	57.2 ± 14.8	52.5 ± 12.8	46.3 ± 12.2
Values and norms	51.2 ± 13.0	45.3 ± 9.7	47.8 ± 10.9	42.9 ± 8.1

Note: Effect of having children: $p = 0.118$ for patients, $p = 0.460$ for spouses.

Table 8.5 provides a comparison of Dyadic Scale ratings, presented also in Figure 8.4. In this analysis, ratings by patients of their relationships with their spouses are compared with the spouses' ratings of their relationships with the patients, with the sample further divided by the presence or absence of children. There is a trend toward a significant effect for the presence or absence of children ($p = 0.071$), with univariate tests being significant at the $p = 0.05$ level for the dimensions of values and norms, control, and involvement. Affective expression

TABLE 8.5.
Self-Dyadic Scale Ratings for Patients and Spouses

FAM Dimensions	Patients—with Children (n = 11)	Patients—No Children (n = 22)	Spouses—with Children (n = 11)	Spouses—No Children (n = 22)
Task accomplished	60.3 ± 19.8	45.6 ± 11.3	47.8 ± 7.0	46.9 ± 8.7
Role performance	59.4 ± 15.8	48.5 ± 10.1	51.2 ± 10.2	49.0 ± 9.8
Communication	55.3 ± 13.7	44.1 ± 9.4	50.1 ± 7.7	46.6 ± 10.0
Affective expression	58.4 ± 12.5	44.9 ± 10.4	51.3 ± 12.4	48.5 ± 8.3
Involvement	57.4 ± 14.8*	47.5 ± 8.6	49.4 ± 11.0	46.0 ± 11.3
Control	60.0 ± 14.4*	47.2 ± 11.2	48.4 ± 7.7	47.7 ± 10.4
Values and norms	54.9 ± 16.6*	45.8 ± 11.1	49.0 ± 7.9	49.5 ± 10.6

Notes:
1. Effect of having children: $p = 0.071$; * = univariate test, $p < 0.05$. Effect of rater (patient, spouse) and interaction effects are not significant.
2. Comparing patients only, effect of having children: $p = 0.096$; all univariate tests significant at $p < 0.05$.

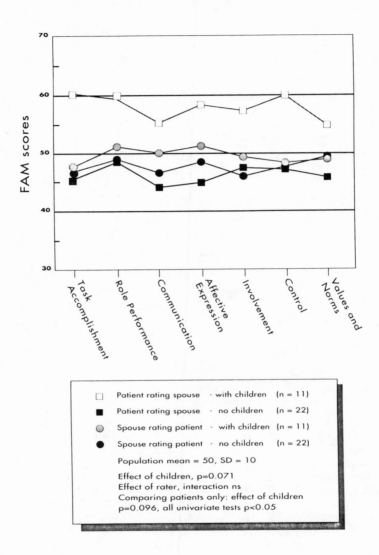

Figure 8.4. FAM Dyadic Scale, for Patients and Spouses, with and without Children

showed a trend toward being significant, at $p = 0.07$. All of the dimensions mentioned above showed that patients who had children reported significant impairment as compared with patients who did not have children. As is the case for WIQ data and for the Self-Rating Scale of the FAM, ratings by spouses do not show an effect of having children. There is no interaction effect. A post hoc analysis was carried out to examine the effect of having children on Dyadic Scale ratings of patients only; the main effect of children in this MANOVA was not significant ($p = 0.096$), with all of the univariate tests being significant at the $p < 0.05$ level.

In summary, most of these observations support the conclusion that patients with or without children report significantly less favorable ratings of marital function than do their spouses. Spouses rate their marriages very close to population norms on both the WIQ and the FAM. This conclusion is most strongly supported by the WIQ data and the Dyadic Scale ratings on the FAM. While one might expect the arrival of children to be associated with some decrease in marital satisfaction, one would expect this view to be shared by both spouses. *The divergent scores of spouses and patients on rating their marriage is perhaps the most compelling evidence these data offer that having children has a detrimental effect on the marriages of patients with eating disorders.* Further, while we have demonstrated elsewhere (Woodside et al., submitted for publication) that there is a significant effect of disordered eating on ratings of family of origin, and to a lesser extent on ratings of current family (see Chapter 7), this explanation cannot be invoked to explain the differences between ratings by the two patient groups (with and without children), both of whom are presumably exposed in a similar fashion to the effects of chaotic eating.

There are numerous reasons why these results must be interpreted with caution. The sample size is rather small, for example, and it may not be representative. Many of the findings on which we commented are only trends statistically and may not persist with a larger sample. Moreover, despite differences in the scores of some measures of marital functioning, there appears to be no difference in the rates of divorce or separation between couples with and without children.

It is interesting to speculate on the meaning of the relatively low rate of childbearing in our sample. While this may simply be an artifact of age or of nutritional status, it may also, at least partially, reflect some awareness at some level that the addition of childbearing would be a strain on the relationship.

IMPLICATIONS FOR CLINICAL MANAGEMENT

The patient with an eating disorder who is also a parent faces a difficult situation. In addition to suffering with a chronic, unremitting, and possibly secret illness, he or she is also confronted with the necessity of providing, possibly as a single parent, for one or more children. In this situation, many factors will serve to exacerbate the patient's chronic sense of inadequacy and ineffectiveness. The enormous shame that the patient experiences around the illness will be amplified by feelings of being inadequate and defective as a parent. This can lead to increasing efforts on the part of the bulimic individual to control the bingeing by dietary restriction, which leads to more bingeing. Patients with AN may be subject to frantic attempts by family members to change behaviors that are ego-syntonic and not especially distressing for the patient, and this can leave the patient feeling abandoned and alone.

Efforts by spouses and families to become substitute caretakers may initially be viewed as helpful, but may also underscore the patient's sense that he or she has no real role in the family and is unnecessary, or that he or she has become too great a burden on the family. In this case, leaving the family may be viewed by the ill individual as an appropriate action. Other patients may adopt a "sick" role, becoming entrenched in a position of helplessness that only feeds into the basic psychopathology of the illness. The same feelings may arise when it is the children who adopt the caretaking role, especially if this happens at a very early age.

As an active eating disorder has a profound effect on any relationship, so too does it affect the marital relationship. Feeling helpless and insecure to begin with, a patient is likely to experience only intensified feelings of being out of control and at the mercy of his or her partner, regardless of the actual quality of the relationship. This situation is particularly tragic, as it is likely that many relationships will improve once eating is normalized.

All of the above put patients at tremendous risk for being drawn into a vicious downward spiral, where their self-perceived deficits in all areas of their lives lead only to intensified self-loathing and further efforts to diet, which makes the behavioral symptoms of the illness worse. Escaping from this downward spiral requires specific treatment, as described in Chapter 1, and is unlikely to occur spontaneously.

When looked at in this light, the patient who is a parent can avoid being viewed as a "good" or a "bad" parent, but instead as an individual who has become caught up in a self-perpetuating cycle of illness, in which there is a marked impairment in all interpersonal relationships, including those with children. Suggesting to such persons that they are bad parents will only accelerate their progress along the downward spiral described above.

The Assessment

If the couple are parents, the marital assessment must contain information about the situation regarding the children. In addition to concrete information, such as what arrangements have been made to care for the children, an inquiry must be directed toward the mechanisms for making decisions about child care, and how each parent (not only the patient) feels about his or her role as a parent. It is important to assess areas of both strengths and weaknesses, as further interventions around parenting will have to be based on areas of perceived strength.

Resources available to the parent must be carefully assessed. It is imperative to evaluate what role the identified patient has taken in relationship to such resources. Are they presented as ctemporary emergency interventions while the patient is recovering? Does the patient have more profound concerns about the ability to return to a more active parenting role? How will these resources respond to the patient's recovery?

We would normally recommend that children be assessed directly. Some patients will insist that their children do not know, or cannot appreciate, the nature of the difficulty. In our own experience, the overwhelming majority of children have been clearly aware that something was wrong, and most identified the problem as somehow related to eating or, in the case of AN, weight. There is a risk, however, that the child who is aware that something is amiss will attribute the problem to himself or herself unless he or she is appropriately informed otherwise. Naturally, the precise nature of the explanation will vary depending on the child's age and level of sophistication. It would be prudent to avoid assuming that the child cannot be aware of eating symptoms, and to ask directly what he or she has noticed about a parent's eating.

Finally, if the family of origin or other resources are being employed to a large extent to care for the children, we would recommend including these individuals in the assessment process at some point, to evaluate the nature of the attachment the children have developed to them.

Interventions to Enhance Parenting Effectiveness

Very Young Children

Interventions aimed at enhancing the patient's sense of effectiveness as a parent will vary depending on the ages of the children and the precise nature of any disturbance they may be experiencing. For very young children, simply bringing them to ccthe treatment setting, introducing them to the treating personnel, and acknowledging that the parent has been ill and is receiving treatment can reduce anxiety dramatically. Observing this reduction tends to be a relief for the parent also, who is likely to feel less guilty and thus more competent in the parenting role.

If the treatment setting allows, eating a meal together with a small child and the patient may be a very concrete way of ascertaining how the child deals with the parent's disorder and of demonstrating to the child that the parent is eating more normally. The less formal setting of a meal also may permit the csmaller child, who may be rather intimidated or shy, to feel more at ease in both asking and answering questions. Finally, if there are any concerns about the child's eating, the meal situation can often clarify these concerns.

It should be emphasized that a decision *not* to parent—that is, to give over the parenting role to another—may be an adaptive decision for some patients while they are in the acute phase of their illness. However, we would view such a decision as a temporary measure, and focus the attention of the couple on when and under what conditions the identified patient would reestablish the parenting role.

Latency-Age Children

Latency-age children are likely to take a more sophisticated view of the affected parent's condition, and usually can comprehend verbal information about the nature of the illness and its treatment. Encouraging the affected parent to direct the child in terms of how he or she can and cannot be of help to the parent will also increase the parent's sense of effectiveness, and perhaps diminish parentification. It is usually important to explain to the child what treatment resources are available to the affected parent, so that the child can feel more confident that he or she can give up the role of caretaker.

The situation in which an older latency-age child has begun to experience alterations in eating habits is very complex. Generally, we avoid focusing too much on such symptoms in family sessions. There are several reasons for this. Practically, it is unlikely that, even if treatment were to be required, it could be effectively delivered at arm's length. Second, the child is the child of the parent, and a therapist who unwisely attempts to cccintervene too strenuously may reinforce the parent's sense of inadequacy and ineffectiveness and put the child in a loyalty bind! The same process can also take place in the mind of the child. It is usually most helpful to use the parent's therapy as a forum for assisting the parent to develop strategies for caring for the child.

Adolescents

The above comments are applicable to older children as well, especially in the case where a teenage child is not overtly engaged in acting out behavior. Adolescents who are using drugs or experiencing other serious behavioral disturbance pose a very difficult problem, and there is no simple way to help a parent of such a child to feel more effective. As distinct from other age groups of children, however, services may be available to which such parents can be referred as an adjunct to the treatment of the eating disorder. A final complication that is more common in this older age group is that adolescence is a period of high risk for the onset of various serious psychiatric illnesses; some of these children may already be in some sort of treatment themselves.

Getting Better for the Children

One statement commonly heard from patients is that the effect of their illness on their children has become so great that they decided to seek treatment to alleviate this suffering. This is an attractive but dangerous rationale for the desperate therapist to accept. Superficially, the lure of improving the lot of children may seem an irresistible lever to use with persons who have a severe eating problem. However, the difficulty that usually arises when using this lever is the same as that encountered whenever a patient chooses to seek treatment to placate someone else: the treatment tends not to belong to the patient, who may come to resent the other person or persons. A further risk of accepting this rationale for treatment is that if the treatment is not successful, the affected parent may feel increasingly ineffective. Finally, parents of adolescents who utilize this rationale successfully may find it difficult to cope with their children's need for increased autonomy and individuation, and so be prone to relapse.

A final issue to consider is the adverse effect on older children of a parent's announcing that he or she is going to recover on the children's behalf, and then is unable to deliver on the promise. On the whole, any potential advantages of this approach appear to be outweighed by its disadvantages.

Blaming the Parent for the Children's Suffering

Many patients with eating disorders are possessed by self-doubt and self-loathing, and find it easy to blame themselves for the suffering of others around them. Some patients will castigate themselves about the suffering of others in an attempt to overcome ambivalence about treatment options or for other reasons. Rarely, therapists, spouses, or family members may fall into the same trap. It is important to emphasize that each individual is responsible for his or her own feelings, and that while parents have a duty to protect their children, an attitude of self-blame is unlikely to be helpful. This stance may be particularly difficult to maintain if there are very serious marital problems and the children are being used as pawns or bargaining chips.

Marital Therapy

We have commented on the high prevalence of marital distress in this particular population. Many such patients will be engaged in marital treatment concurrently with or as a follow-up to shorter-term treatment that focuses more narrowly on eating issues. We believe that it is important for children of such parents to have a clear understanding, suitable to their age and cognitive ability, of the purpose of the treatment, its expected benefits, and how they are expected to be involved or not involved in the process.

Marital therapists who do not have family assessment skills or who choose not to assess the families of couples they treat might be advised to consider arranging for such an assessment to be performed. Information that is critical is the presence or absence of alliances between the children and each parent, and an evaluation of how it is thought that the structure of the family might be affected if the patient were to develop more normal eating habits.

It is often the case that, because of the eating disorders, one parent effectively has become the sole parent for the children in question. It is possible that there will be resistance to the affected parent's resuming a more active role in parenting; in fact, often the affected parent has been ill throughout the entire relationship, and has never taken an equal role in parenting. Negotiating this type of issue may represent an important challenge for some couples.

It unfortunately is true that, despite the best efforts of all concerned, some marriages will fail, either by mutual choice or by a unilateral action of one of the partners. The parent with an active or recovered eating disorder is vulnerable to being unable to act in a decisive or effective manner in the face of such a situation, and may need the support of an independent third party, such as an individual therapist. Children of all ages may also require considerable support, as well; the child who should inspire the most concern may be the child who appears to be unconcerned about the impending or actual separation, or the child who is most involved in supporting the affected parent and neglecting his or her own well-being.

A rare issue that will surface is physical or sexual abuse of a child of a patient with an eating disorder, either by the nonaffected spouse or by the eating-disordered parent. In this case, the individual therapist must act in accordance with local laws regarding such situations. For example, in the province of Ontario, physicians, social workers, and many other professionals are required to report even the suspicion of child abuse to the local Children's Aid Society, or face stiff legal penalties. However, regardless of the legal guidelines of a specific locale, we feel that the situation warrants immediate action on the part of the therapist to refer the child to whatever agency is responsible for the assessment of children at risk for sexual and physical abuse.

Involvement of Family of Origin

Assessment of the family of origin may be a crucial element in assisting the patient who is a parent, particularly if grandparents or aunts/uncles are involved in the care of the children. Issues similar to those raised in the preceding two sections apply equally well to families of origin.

SUMMARY

It is not surprising to find that eating disorders, like any chronic ill-ness, have profound effects on one's psychosocial functioning, including the ability to parent. Nor is it surprising to learn that the quality of a patient's marriage might affect his or her perception of the ability to parent effectively. But for patients with eating disorders, there is a significant set of ironies unique to the nature of the illness. The first is the profound effect that perceived disappointment and failure have on the very symptoms of the eating disorders (that is, intensification of the dieting behavior), and the second is the paradox that many patients appear to be functioning at a much higher level than is actually the case, and thus are subject to being deprived inadvertently of needed assistance.

It also is not surprising that many would wish that children in such situations could remain unaware of and be unaffected by the events around them. Sadly, however, this is not the case. We feel that an empathic, understanding approach to both persons with eating disor-ders and their children will help to ameliorate the suffering.

References and Bibliography

American Psychiatric Association (1987). *Diagnostic and statistical manual of mental disorders* (3rd ed., rev.). Washington, D.C.: Author.

Andersen, A. E. (1985). *Practical comprehensive treatment of anorexia and bulimia* (pp. 135–148, 160–164). Baltimore: Johns Hopkins University Press.

Barrett, M. J., & Schwartz, R. (1987). Couple therapy for bulimia. *Family Therapy Collections, 20,* 25–39.

Beckman, K. A., & Burns, L. G. (1990). Relation of sexual abuse and bulimia in college women. *International Journal of Eating Disorders, 9,* 487–492.

Beumont, P. J. V., Abraham, S. F., & Simon, K. (1981). The psychosexual histories of adolescent girls and young women with anorexia nervosa. *Psychological Medicine, 11,* 131–140.

Boszormenyi-Nagy, I., & Krasner, B. (1986). *Between give and take: A clinical guide to contextual therapy.* New York: Brunner/Mazel.

Boszormenyi-Nagy, I., & Sparkes, G. (1973). *Invisible loyalties: Reciprocity in intergenerational family therapy.* New York: Harper & Row.

Bowen, M. (1978). *Family therapy in clinical practice.* New York: Aronson

Bowlby, J. (1977a). The making and breaking of affectional bonds. I. Aetiology and psychopathology in the light of attachment theory. *British Journal of Psychiatry, 130,* 201–210.

Bowlby, J. (1977b). The making and breaking of affectional bonds. II. Some principles of psychopathology. *British Journal of Psychiatry, 130,* 421–431.

Bowlby, J. (1982). Attachment and loss: Retrospect and prospect. *American Journal of Orthopsychiatry, 52,* 664–678.

Brandes, J. (1991). Outpatient family therapy for bulimia nervosa. In D. B. Woodside & L. F. Shekter-Wolfson (Eds.), *Family approaches in treatment of eating disorders* (pp. 49–66). Washington, D.C.: American Psychiatric Press.

Brinch, M., Isager, T., & Tolstrup, K. (1988). Anorexia nervosa and motherhood:

Reproductional pattern and mothering behavior of 50 women. *Acta Psychiatrica Scandinavica*, 77, 98–104.

Brink, T. L. (1979). *Geriatric psychotherapy*. New York: Human Services Press.

Brown, A., & Finkelhor, D. (1986). Impact of child sexual abuse: A review of the research. *Psychological Bulletin*, 99, 66–77.

Bulik, C., Sullivan, P., & Rorty, M. (1989). Childhood sexual abuse in women with bulimia. *Journal of Clinical Psychiatry*, 49, 7–9.

Byng-Hall, J. (1988). Scripts and legends in families and family therapy. *Family Process*, 27, 167–179.

Byng-Hall, J (1990): Attachment theory and family therapy. *Infant Mental Health Journal*, 11:228-236.

Calam, R. M., & Slade, P. D. (1989). Sexual experience and eating problems in female undergraduates. *International Journal of Eating Disorders, 8*, 391–397.

Ciliska, D. (1991). *Beyond dieting*. New York: Brunner/Mazel.

Cooper, P. J., & Fairburn, C. G. (1987). The eating disorder examination: A semi-structured interview for the assessment of the specific psychopathology of eating disorders. *International Journal of Eating Disorders, 6*, 1–8.

Courtois, C. A. (1988). *Healing the incest wound*. New York: Norton.

Crisp, A. (1980). *Anorexia nervosa: Let me be*. London: Academic.

Crisp, A. H. (1977). Diagnosis and outcome of anorexia nervosa: The St. George's view. *Proceedings of the Royal Society of Medicine, 70*, 464–470.

Crisp, A. H., Harding, B., & McGuiness, B. (1974). Anorexia nervosa. Psychoneurotic characteristics of parents: Relationship to prognosis. A quantitative study. *Journal of Psychosomatic Research, 18*, 167–173.

Crisp, A. H., Kalucy, R. S., Lacey, J. H., & Harding, B. (1977). The long-term prognosis in anorexia nervosa: Some factors predictive of outcome, In R. A. Vigersky (Ed.), *Anorexia nervosa* (pp. 55–65). New York: Raven.

Crisp, A. H., Norton, K., Gowers, S., Halek, C., Bowyer, C., Yeldham, D., Levett, G., & Bhat, A. (1991). A controlled study of the effect of therapies aimed at adolescent and family psychopathology in anorexia nervosa. *British Journal of Psychiatry, 159*, 335–343.

Crisp, A. H., Palmer, R. L., & Kalucy, R. S. (1976). How common is anorexia nervosa? A prevalence study. *British Journal of Psychiatry, 218*, 549–554.

Dally, P. (1984). Anorexia tardive—late onset marital anorexia nervosa. *Journal of Psychosomatic Research, 28*, 423–428.

Davis, R., & Olmsted, M. P. (1992). Cognitive-behavioral group treatment for bulmia nervosa: Integrating psychoeducation and psychotherapy. In H. Harper-Giuffre & K. R. MacKenzie (Eds), *Group psychotherapy for eating disorders* (pp. 71–104). Washington, D.C.: American Psychiatric Press.

Doherty, W., & Colangelo, N. (1984). The family FIRO model: A modest proposal for organizing family treatment. *Journal of Marital and Family Therapy, 10,* 19–29.

Doherty, W. J., Colangelo, N., Green, A. M., & Hoffman, G. S. (1985). Emphases of the major family therapy models: A family FIRO analysis. *Journal of Marital and Family Therapy, 11,* 299–303.

Doherty, W. J., & Harkaway, J. E. (1990). Obesity and family systems: A family FIRO approach to assessment and treatment planning. *Journal of Marital and Family Therapy, 16,* 287– 298.

Epstein, N. B., Rakoff, V., & Sigal, T. T. (1968). *Family categories schema.* Montreal: McGill University.

Fairburn, C. G. (1988). The current status of the psychological treatments for bulimia nervosa. *Journal of Psychosomatic Research, 32,* 635–645.

Fairburn C. G., & Beglin, S. J. (1990). Studies of the epidemiology of bulimia nervosa. *American Journal of Psyhiatry, 147,* 401–408.

Feingold, M., Kaminer, Y., Lyons, K., Chaudhury, A. K., Costigan, K., & Cetrulo, C. L. (1988). Bulimia nervosa in pregnancy: A case report. *Obstetrics and Gynecology, 71,* 1025–1027.

Fichter, M. M., & Pirke, K. M. (1984). Hypothalamic-pituitary function in starving healthy subjects. In K. M. Pirke & D. Ploog (Eds.), *The psychobiology of anorexia nervosa.* New York: Springer-Verlag.

Fishman, H. C. (1979). Family considerations in liaison psychiatry, a structural approach to anorexia nervosa in adults. *Psychiatric Clinics of North America, 2,* 249–263.

Fossum, M. A., & Mason, M. J. (1986). *Facing shame: Families in recovery.* New York: Norton.

Foster, S. W. (1986). Marital treatment of eating disorders. In N. S. Jacobson & A. S. Gurman (Eds.), *Clinical handbook of marital therapy* (pp. 575–593). New York: Guilford.

Garfinkel, P. E., & Garner, D. M. (1982). *Anorexia nervosa: A multidimensional perspective.* New York: Brunner/Mazel.

Garfinkel, P. E., & Garner, D. M. (Eds.) (1987). *The role of drug treatments for eating disorders.* New York: Brunner/Mazel.

Garfinkel P. E., Garner, D. M., Rose, J., Darby, P. L., Brandes, J. S., O'Hanlon, J., & Walsh, N. (1983). A comparison of characteristics of families of patients with anorexia nervosa and normal controls. *Psychological Medicine, 13,* 821–828.

Garfinkel, P. E., Moldofsky, H., & Garner, D. M. (1980). The heterogeneity of anorexia nervosa. *Archives of General Psychiatry, 37,* 1036–1040.

Garner, D., & Garfinkel, P. E. (1985). *Handbook of psychotherapy for anorexia nervosa and bulimia.* New York: Guilford.

Gelinas, D. J. (1983). The persisting negative effect of incest. *Psychiatry*, *46*, 312–332.

Goldbloom, D. S., Kennedy, S. H., Kaplan, A. S., & Woodside, D. B. (1989). Recent advances in pharmacotherapy: Anorexia nervosa and bulimia nervosa. *Canadian Medical Association Journal*, *140*, 1149–1154.

Goldfarb, L.A. (1987). Sexual abuse antecedent to anorexia nervosa, bulimia and compulsive overeating: Three case reports. *International Journal of Eating Disorders*, *6*, 675–680.

Guile, L., Horne, M., & Dunster, R. (1978). Anorexia nervosa, sexual behaviour modification as an adjunct to an integrated treatment program: A case report. *Australian and New Zealand Journal of Psychiatry*, *12*, 165–167.

Haley, J. (1976). *Problem-solving therapy: New strategies for effective family therapy*. San Francisco: Jossey-Bass.

Hall, R., Tice, L., Beresford, T., Wooley, B., & Hall, A. K. (1989). Sexual abuse in patients with anorexia nervosa and bulimia. *Psychosomatics*, *30*, 73–79.

Heavey, A., Parker, Y., Bhat, A. V., Crisp, A. H., & Growers, S. G. (1989). Anorexia nervosa and marriage. *International Journal of Eating Disorders*, *8*, 275–284.

Hedblom, J. E., Hubbard, F. A., & Andersen, A. E. (1982). Anorexia nervosa: A multidisciplinary treatment program for patient and family. *Social Work in Health Care*, *12*, 238–248.

Herman, J. L. (1981). *Father-daughter incest*. Cambridge, Mass.: Harvard University Press.

Herzog, D. B. (1982). Bulimia: The secretive syndrome. *Psychosomatics*, *23*, 481–487.

Hsu, L. K., & Zimmer, B. (1988). Eating disorders in old age. *International Journal of Eating Disorders*, *7*, 133–138.

Hsu, L. K. G., Crisp, A. H., & Harding, B. (1979). Outcome of anorexia nervosa. *Lancet*, *1*, 61–65.

Huon, G. (1985). Bulimia: Therapy at a distance. In S. W. Trouyz & P. J. V. Beaumont (Eds.), *Eating disorders prevalence and treatment* (pp. 62–73). Sydney: Williams & Wilkins.

Igoin-Apfelbaum, L. (1985). Characteristics of family background in bulimia. *Psychotherapy and Psychosomatics*, *43*, 161–167.

Jonas, J. M., Pope, H. G., Hudson, J. I., & Satlin, A. (1984). Undiagnosed vomiting in an older woman: Unsuspected bulimia. *American Journal of Psychiatry*, *141*, 902–903.

Kaplan, A. S., & Woodside, D. B. (1987). Biologic aspects of anorexia nervosa and bulimia. *Journal of Clinical and Consulting Psychology*, *55*, 645–53.

Kapoor, S. A., (1989). Help for the significant others of bulimia. *Journal of Applied Social Psychology*, *19*, 50–66.

Kearney-Cooke, A. (1988). Group treatment of sexual abuse among women with eating disorders. *Women's Therapy, 7*, 5–21.

Kellet, J., Trimble, M., & Thorley, A. (1976). Anorexia nervosa after menopause. *British Journal of Psychiatry, 128*, 555–558.

Kerr, A. G., & Piran, N. (1990). Comprehensive group treatment program. In N. Piran & A. S. Kaplan (Eds.), *A Day Hospital group treatment program for anorexia nervosa and bulimia nervosa* (pp. 20–41). New York: Brunner/Mazel.

Keys, A., Brozek, J., Henschel, A., Mickelson, O., & Taylor, H. L. (1950). *The biology of human starvation*. Minneapolis: University of Minnesota Press.

Kog, E., & Vandereycken, W. (1985). Family characteristics of anorexia nervosa and bulimia: A review of the research literature. *Clinical Psychology Review, 5*, 159–180.

Kwee, M. G. T., & Duivenvoorden, H. L. (1985). Multimodal residential therapy in two cases of anorexia nervosa (adult body weight phobia). In A. A. Lazarus (Ed.), *Casebook of multimodal therapy* (pp. 116–138). New York: Guilford.

Lacey, H., & Smith, G. (1987). Bulimia nervosa: The impact of pregnancy on mother and baby. *British Journal of Psychiatry, 150*, 777–781.

Lacey, J. H. (1983). Bulimia nervosa, binge eating and psychogenic vomiting: A controlled treatment study and long-term outcome. *British Medical Journal, 286*, 1609–1613.

Lacey, J. H. (1985). Time-limited individual and group treatment for bulimia. In D. Garner & P. Garfinkel (Eds.), *Handbook of psychotherapy for anorexia nervosa and bulimia* (pp. 431–457). New York: Guilford.

Launer, M. A. (1978). Anorexia nervosa in late life. *British Journal of Medical Psychology, 51*, 375–377.

Leichner, P. P., Harper, D. E., & Johnson, D. M. (1985). Adjunctive group support for spouses of women with anorexia nervosa and/or bulimia. *International Journal of Eating Disorders, 4*, 227–235.

Levine, P. (1988). "Bulimic" couples: Dynamics and treatment. *Family Therapy Collections, 25*, 89–104.

Lewis, H. B. (1987). The role of shame in depression over the life span. In H. B. Lewis (Ed.), *The role of shame in symptom formation* (pp. 29–50). Hillsdale, N.J.: Erlbaum.

Madanes, C. (1981). *Strategic family therapy*. San Francisco: Jossey-Bass.

McGoldrick, M., & Gerson, R. (1985). *Genograms in family assessment*. New York: Norton.

Milner, G., & O'Leary, M. M. (1988). Anorexia nervosa occurring in pregnancy. *Acta Psychiatrica Scandinavica, 77*, 491–492.

Minuchin, S. (1974). *Families and family therapy*. Cambridge, Mass.: Harvard University Press.

Minuchin, S., Rosman, B. L., & Baker, L. (1978). *Psychosomatic families: Anorexia nervosa in context*. Cambridge, Mass.: Harvard University Press.

Morgan, H. G., & Russell, G. F. M. (1975). Value of family background and clinical features as predictors of long-term outcome in anorexia nervosa: Four-year follow-up study of 41 patients. *Psychological Medicine, 5*, 355–371.

Nathanson, D. L. (1992). *Shame and pride: Affect, sex, and the birth of the self*. New York: Norton.

Nichols, M. (1984). *Family therapy: Concepts and methods*. New York: Gardner.

Oppenheimer, R., Howells, K., Palmer, R. L., & Chaloner, D. A. (1985). Adverse sexual experiences in childhood and clinical eating disorders: A preliminary description. *Journal of Psychiatric Research, 19*, 357–361.

Oyewumi, L. K. (1981). Is anorexia nervosa a disease of all ages? *Psychiatric Journal of the University of Ottawa, 6*, 39– 42.

Piran, N., & Kaplan, A. S. (Eds.) (1990). *A Day Hospital treatment for eating disorders*. New York: Brunner/Mazel.

Pittman, F. (1989). *Private lives: Infidelity and the betrayal of intimacy*. New York: Norton.

Polivy, J. (1976). Perception of calories and regulation of intake in restrained and unrestrained subjects. *Addictive Behaviours, 1*, 237–243.

Roberto, L. G. (1986). Bulimia: The transgenerational view. *Journal of Marital and Family Therapy, 12*, 231–240.

Roberto, L. G. (1987). Bulimia: Transgenerational family therapy. *Family Therapy Collections, 20*, 1–11.

Roberto, L. G. (1991). Impasses in the family treatment of bulimia. In D. B. Woodside & L. Shekter-Wolfson (Eds.), *Family approaches in treatment of eating disorders* (pp. 67–85). Washington, D.C.: American Psychiatric Press.

Root, M. P., & Fallon, P. (1988). The incidence of victimization experience in a bulimic sample. *Journal of Interpersonal Violence, 3*, 161–173.

Root, M. P., Fallon, P., & Friedrick, W. N. (1986). *Bulimia: A systems approach to treatment*. New York: Norton.

Russell, G. F. M. (1979). Bulimia nervosa: An ominous variant of anorexia nervosa. *Psychological Medicine, 9*, 429–448.

Russell, G. F. M., Szmukler, G. I., Dare, C., & Eisler, I. (1987). An evaluation of family therapy in anorexia nervosa and bulimia nervosa. *Archives of General Psychiatry, 44*, 1047– 1056.

Schechter, J. O., Schwartz, H. P., & Greenfield, D. G. (1987). Sexual assault and anorexia nervosa. *International Journal of Eating Disorders, 6*, 313–316.

Schwartz, R. C., Barrett, M. J., & Saba, G. (1985). Family therapy for bulimia. In D. M. Garner & P. E. Garfinkel (Eds.), *Handbook of psychotherapy for anorexia nervosa and bulimia* (pp. 280–307). New York: Guilford.

Selvini-Palazzoli, M. (1978). *Self-starvation: From individual to family therapy in the treatment of anorexia nervosa*. New York: Aronson.

Selvini-Palazzoli, M., Boscolo, L., Cecchin, G., & Prata, G. (1978). *Paradox and Counterparadox*. New York: Aronson.

Selvini-Palazzoli, M., & Viaro, M. (1988). The anorectic process in the family: A six-stage model as a guide for individual therapy. *Family Process, 27*, 129–148.

Shekter-Wolfson, L., & Kennedy, S. (1991). Integrating individual and family therapy in an in-patient eating disorders unit. In D. B. Woodside & L. Shekter-Wolfson (Eds.), *Family approaches in treatment of eating disorders* (pp. 123–140). Washington, D.C.: American Psychiatric Press.

Shekter-Wolfson, L., & Woodside, D. B. (1990). Family treatment. In N. Piran & A. S. Kaplan (Eds.), *A Day Hospital treatment of eating disorders* (pp. 79–109). New York: Brunner/Mazel.

Shekter-Wolfson, L., & Woodside, D. B. (1991). A family relations group. In D. B. Woodside & L. Shekter-Wolfson (Eds.), *Family approaches in treatment of eating disorders* (pp. 107–122). Washington, D.C.: American Psychiatric Press.

Silberstein, L. R., Striegel-Moore, R., & Rodin, J. (1987). Feeling fat: A woman's shame. In H. B. Lewis (Ed.), *The role of shame in symptom formation* (pp. 89–108). Hillsdale, N.J.: Erlbaum.

Skinner, H. A., Steinhauer, P. D., & Santa-Barbara, J. (1983). The family assessment measure. *Canadian Journal of Community Mental Health, 2*, 91–105.

Sloan, G., & Leichner, P. (1986). Is there a relationship between sexual abuse or incest and eating disorders? *Canadian Journal of Psychiatry, 31*, 656–660.

Steinhauer, P. D., Santa-Barbara, J., & Skinner, H. (1984). The process model of family functioning. *Canadian Journal of Psychiatry, 29*, 77–88.

Stewart, D. E., Raskin, J., Garfinkel, P. E., MacDonald, O. L., & Robinson, G. E. (1987). Anorexia nervosa, bulimia and pregnancy. *American Journal of Obstetrics and Gynecology, 157*, 1194–1198.

Stierlin, H., & Weber, G. (1989). *Unlocking the family door: A systemic approach to the understanding and treatment of anorexia nervosa*. New York: Brunner/Mazel.

Strober, M., & Katz, J. L. (1988). Depression in the eating disorders: A review and analysis of descriptive, family, and biological findings. In D. M. Garner, & P. E. Garfinkel (Eds.), *Diagnostic issues in anorexia nervosa and bulimia nervosa* (pp. 88–111). New York: Brunner/Mazel.

Treasure, J. L., & Russell, G. F. M. (1988). Intrauterine growth and neonatal weight gain in babies of women with anorexia nervosa (letter). *British Medical Journal, 296*, 1038.

Van Buren, D. J., & Williamson, D. A. (1988). Marital relationships and conflict resolution skills of bulimics. *International Journal of Eating Disorders, 7*, 735–741.

Van den Broucke, S., & Vandereycken, W. (1989a). The marital relationship of patients with an eating disorder: A questionnaire study. *International Journal of Eating Disorders, 8,* 541–556.

Van den Broucke, S., & Vandereyckyen, W. (1989b). Eating disorders in married patients: Theory and therapy. In W. Vandereycken, E. Kog, & J. Vandirlinden (Eds.), *The family approach to eating disorders* (pp. 333–345). New York: PMA.

Van den Broucke, S., & Vandereycken, W. (1989c). Eating disorder in married patients: A comparison with unmarried anorexia and an exploration of the marital relationship. In W. Vandereycken, E. Kog, and J. Vanderlinden (Eds.), *The family approach to eating disorders* (pp. 173–188). New York: PMA.

Vandereycken, W. (1988). Anorexia nervosa in adults. In B. J. Blinder, B. F. Chaitlin, & R. Goldstein (Eds.), *The eating disorders* (pp. 295–304). New York: PMA.

Vandereycken, W., & Pierloot, R. (1983). Long-term outcome research in anorexia nervosa. The problem of patient selection and follow-up duration. *International Journal of Eating Disorders, 2,* 237–242.

Waller, G. (1991). Sexual abuse as a factor in eating disorders. *British Journal of Eating Disorders, 159,* 664–671.

Waring, E. M. (1985). Measurement of intimacy: Conceptual and methodological issues of studying close relationships. *Psychological Medicine, 15,* 9–14.

Waring E. M., & Reddon J. (1983): The measurement of intimacy in marriage: The Waring Questionnaire. *Journal of Clinical Psychology, 39:* 53–57.

Willis, D. C., & Rand, C. S. (1988). Pregnancy in bulimic women. *Obstetrics and Gynecology, 71,* 708–710.

Woodman, M. (1982). *Addiction to perfection: The still unravished bride.* Toronto: Inner City Books.

Woodside, D. B., & Garfinkel, P. E. (1992). Age of onset of eating disorders. *International Journal of Eating Disorders, 12,* 31–36.

Woodside, D. B., & Shekter-Wolfson, L. F. (1990). Parenting by patients with anorexia nervosa and bulimia nervosa. *International Journal of Eating Disorders, 9,* 303–309.

Woodside, D. B., & Shekter-Wolfson, L. (1991). Family treatment in the Day Hospital. In D. B. Woodside & L. Shekter-Wolfson (Eds.), *Family approaches in treatment of eating disorders* (pp. 87–105). Washington, D.C.: American Psychiatric Press.

Woodside, D. B., Shekter-Wolfson, L. F., Garfinkel, P. E., Olmsted, M. P., & Kaplan, A. S. *Family functioning in bulimia nervosa I.* Submitted for publication.

Name Index

Abraham, S., 24
American Psychiatric Association, 1
Andersen, A., 24, 35, 36, 40, 41, 42, 51, 53, 61, 86, 103, 105, 113, 121, 125, 127, 128, 163

Baker, L., 58
Barrett, M., 25, 27, 28, 30, 32, 40, 41, 42, 43, 44, 45, 46, 50
Beckman, K., 33, 34
Beglin, S., 5
Beumont, P., 24, 33
Boszormenyi-Nagy, I., 123, 131, 132
Bowen, M., 89
Bowlby, J., 60, 61
Brandes, J., 60
Brinch, M., 38, 39
Brown, A., 34
Bulik, C., 33
Burns, L., 33, 34
Byng-Hall, J., 132

Calam, R., 33
Cooper, P., 9
Courtois, C., 34
Crisp, A., 4, 24, 25, 31, 33, 34, 52, 53, 163

Dally, P., 5, 24, 25, 26, 29, 35, 36, 37, 52, 53, 163
Davis, R., 15
Doherty, W., 105, 106

Duivenvoorden, H., 28, 40, 53
Dunster, R., 33

Epstein, N., 138

Fairburn, C., 5, 9
Fallon, P., 27, 33, 34, 63
Feingold, M., 38
Fichter, M., 1
Finkelhor, D., 34
Fishman, H., 27, 28, 53
Fossum, M., 64, 68, 124
Foster, S., 24, 25, 27, 28, 37, 40, 41, 42, 43, 44, 96
Friedrick, W., 27

Garfinkel, P., 5, 12, 20, 24, 61, 78
Garner, D., 5, 12, 20, 24, 78
Gelinas, D., 74
Gerson, R., 91
Goldbloom, D., 20
Goldfarb, L., 34
Greenfield, D., 33
Guile, L., 33

Haley, J., 103, 104, 113
Hall, R., 33
Harding, B., 33
Harkaway, J., 105, 106
Harper, D., 53
Heavey, A., 23, 24, 33, 35
Hedblom, J., 24, 40
Herman, J., 34

Subject Index